LUKE MANGAN

SHARING PLATES

ACKNOWLEDGMENTS

Firstly, a big thank you must go to my Group Head Chef, Joe Pavlovich, for making this book come to life; from working with me on the recipe creation and testing, right through to the final photography. There are some amazing recipes in this book, some inspired by our travels, but most served in our restaurants today, from our founding restaurant glass brasserie, to Salt tapas in Singapore and soon Ginza, Tokyo. Joe is one of my longest serving chefs and I can't thank him enough for his commitment to this company.

A huge thank you to Rebecca McNeilly, my amazing PA (jack of all trades and master of all) for also working so closely with Joe on every detail of this book.

A big thank you to all my restaurant staff, from chefs, waiters and bar staff to our restaurant managers: your passion and service to provide our customers with the best dining experience possible does not go unnoticed.

To my head office staff who keep the wheels rolling behind the scenes: your integrity and loyalty to the Luke Mangan brand has helped to make this company what it is to today.

To my partners in Australia and overseas — Hilton Hotels, Virgin Australia, Volvo, P&O Cruises, Electrolux and Trippas White Group — I thank you for your ongoing support of our company and we look forward to continuing our great partnerships for many more years to come.

LUKE MANGAN

SHARING PLATES

for brunch, lunch and dinner with friends

MURDOCH BOOKS

SYDNEY · LONDON

Introduction 7

Breakfast & Brunch 10

Bread 38

Snacks & Salads 56

Oysters & Sashimi 82

Fish & Shellfish 98

Meat 130

Poultry 168

Sweets 192

Basics 224
Index 234

INTRODUCTION

There is something truly satisfying about sharing good food at a table with family and friends. While formal dining will always have its place, many people are steering away from the traditional notion of sitting down to a three-course meal of starter, main dish and dessert, and are instead embracing a more laid-back style of eating, sharing a few different plates of food.

This way of eating is nothing new, of course — the Spanish, with their countless tapas bars, have been excelling at it for centuries. So have the Chinese, with dim sum or yum cha, the Koreans with their banchan and the Indians with their thali. Scandinavians are known for their smorgasbords, the Middle Easterns enjoy meze plates and the Italians are famous for antipasti.

And why not? Sharing food creates interaction and conversation at the table, allowing diners to explore more tastes and flavours in one sitting.

When choosing a selection of shared dishes for a gathering, think about balancing flavours and textures, how much time you have for preparation and what elements of the menu can be made well in advance, leaving you free to enjoy some leisurely grazing and feasting. A selection of tasty fingerfoods, or a platter of oysters, sashimi or tapas-type nibbles, is perfect for sharing if you are having people over for a few drinks. To avoid a confusion of flavours, and to keep menu planning easy, it's often simplest to stick to a general style of cuisine, for example Asian, Spanish or Mediterranean — but don't be afraid to be a bit adventurous too.

This book offers a whole range of great ideas for shared plates, from leisurely breakfasts and elegant brunches to warming winter dishes and light, lazy summer fare, to bar snacks and fun, informal foods to enjoy with a bunch of friends. Whatever the occasion, you're sure to find something perfect for sharing.

Chapter 1
Breakfast & Brunch

At the end of a long working week, there's something quite ceremonious about sharing a leisurely weekend breakfast or brunch with family and friends, whether it's at home at the kitchen bench or at a favourite café. In this busy day and age, many of us, most working days, just grab a quick breakfast on the run, or even skip it altogether in our rush to dash out the door — making it all the more special when we're able to enjoy a lingering morning repast with family and friends. When I'm at home, mid-week breakfast is pretty basic, such as a simple bowl of oats with a nice cup of tea or a strong coffee — but at the weekend it's a whole different story.

Most recipes in this chapter can be enjoyed for both breakfast and brunch. And they're not necessarily time consuming to pull together, such as our jazzed-up toasted sandwich (page 23), shakshuka (page 24) and granola (page 35). For summer mornings there's a beautiful chilled chia custard (page 20), or zucchini fritters with smoked salmon (page 30). And in many recipes, various elements can be made in advance — such as the pico de gallo and kimchi mayo for the crispy egg and bacon tacos (page 21) — and simply assembled when guests arrive.

But don't be limited to the recipes in this chapter: you'll find so many brunch-style dishes throughout this book, such as the English muffins with swordfish on page 103. All very lovely ways to ease into the day.

What an elegant way to start the day. Don't be fooled by their tiny size — quail eggs are beautifully rich in flavour. Most good butchers will stock them.

Quail eggs benedict with chilli kale on mini muffins

MAKES 8

FOR THE HOLLANDAISE REDUCTION Heat a saucepan over low heat with a splash of olive oil. Add the shallot and garlic and cook gently for 2–3 minutes without browning. Add the remaining ingredients, except the fresh tarragon, and allow to reduce by three-quarters. Add the fresh tarragon and remove from the heat.

Cover with plastic wrap and cool overnight in the fridge. Strain, discarding the solids. (You only need 2 tablespoons for the hollandaise; the rest will keep in an airtight container in the fridge for up to 6 months.)

FOR THE HOLLANDAISE SAUCE Place the egg yolks and hollandaise reduction in a clean metal bowl. Set the bowl over a saucepan of simmering water, ensuring the base of the bowl doesn't touch the water. Begin whisking at 30 second intervals, taking the bowl on and off the heat (so it doesn't get too hot), until the mixture holds a 'figure eight' for more than 6 seconds.

Slowly add the clarified butter, whisking constantly; add a little hot water if the mixture is too thick. Stir in the cayenne pepper and lemon juice, and season with salt and pepper. Keep in a warm place, covering the surface with plastic wrap to prevent a skin forming.

FOR THE CHILLI KALE Warm the olive oil in a frying pan over medium heat. Cook the shallot for 1–2 minutes. Add the kale and cook for 2–3 minutes. Stir in the chilli paste and cook for 2 minutes. Season and keep warm.

TO SERVE In a large frying pan over medium heat, fry the quail eggs in a drizzle of olive oil, sunny side up. Top the warm toasted muffin halves with the kale, a slice of ham and a quail egg. Season, dollop with hollandaise and briefly warm under a hot grill. Enjoy immediately.

4 English muffins (page 54), split in half and toasted
splash of olive oil
8 quail eggs
8 thin slices double-smoked ham
150 ml (5 fl oz) Hollandaise sauce (see below)

HOLLANDAISE REDUCTION
extra virgin olive oil, for pan-frying
3 French shallots, chopped
2 garlic cloves, sliced
300 ml (10½ fl oz) white wine
500 ml (17 fl oz/2 cups) white wine vinegar
2 teaspoons dried tarragon
4 bay leaves
1 teaspoon white peppercorns
½ bunch tarragon

HOLLANDAISE SAUCE
4 egg yolks
2 tablespoons Hollandaise reduction (see above)
300 ml (10½ fl oz) warm melted clarified butter or ghee
pinch of cayenne pepper
juice of 1 lemon

CHILLI KALE
3 tablespoons extra virgin olive oil
4 French shallots, finely diced
4 large curly kale leaves, chopped
1 teaspoon chilli paste

These tarts are indulgent enough, but if you'd really like to impress, use jamón instead of pancetta. Jamón is much more expensive, but the flavour is worth it.

Pancetta & onion tarts with asparagus, buffalo mozzarella & honey thyme dressing

MAKES 4

50 g (1¾ oz) unsalted butter
2 large onions, cut into thin slices
80 ml (2½ fl oz/⅓ cup) thick (double) cream (55% fat)
4 thyme sprigs, leaves picked, plus extra to garnish
plain (all-purpose) flour, for dusting
300 g (10½ oz) ready-made puff pastry
1 egg yolk, beaten
24 thin slices pancetta
3 buffalo mozzarella balls, each cut into 4 pieces
12 asparagus spears, peeled if not tender, blanched
handful wild rocket (arugula)

HONEY THYME DRESSING
100 ml (3½ fl oz) honey
100 ml (3½ fl oz) chardonnay
½ bunch thyme, plus an extra 1 tablespoon thyme leaves
150 ml (5 fl oz) extra virgin olive oil

FOR THE HONEY THYME DRESSING Combine the honey, chardonnay, thyme and 200 ml (7 fl oz) water in a saucepan over medium heat. Bring to a simmer and allow to reduce by one-third. Cool slightly, strain into a bowl, then slowly whisk in the olive oil, ensuring the honey is still warm so the oil will emulsify. Add the extra thyme leaves and set aside.

FOR THE TARTS Melt the butter in a heavy-based pan over low heat. Add the onion and cook gently for 45 minutes, without colouring, stirring every 10 minutes. Stir in the cream and thyme leaves and simmer for another 20 minutes, until the liquid has reduced by three-quarters. Season to taste and transfer to a bowl.

On a floured bench, roll out the pastry 3–4 mm (³⁄₁₆ inch) thick. Transfer to a tray, cover with plastic wrap and chill for 30 minutes. Cut the pastry into four 8 x 14 cm (3¼ x 5½ inch) rectangles. Return to the tray, cover again and chill for a further 15 minutes.

Preheat the oven to 170°C (325°F). Place the pastry pieces on a baking tray lined with baking paper. Prick each five or six times with a fork, then spread with the onion mixture, leaving a 1 cm (½ inch) border on all sides. Brush the borders with the egg yolk. Divide the pancetta among the pastry rectangles.

Bake for 20 minutes, pushing the tarts down with a spatula several times to stop them rising in the middle. Remove the tray from the oven and carefully turn the tarts over. Bake for another 10–20 minutes, or until well cooked and crisp. Cool slightly, then turn over again.

TO SERVE Place the tarts on serving plates and top with the mozzarella and asparagus. Season, add the rocket, drizzle with the honey thyme dressing and serve.

Here is a great vegetarian breakfast dish, with lots of beautiful Moroccan spices. Sweet potato also works well instead of the pumpkin.

Smashed spiced pumpkin & ricotta on rye with poached eggs

MAKES 8

8 free-range eggs
3 tablespoons vinegar
1 teaspoon salt
8 slices rye bread, toasted
3 tablespoons dukkah (a blend of toasted nuts and spices, available from good food stores)
½ bunch chives, finely chopped
8 thyme sprigs, leaves picked
extra virgin olive oil, for drizzling

MOROCCAN-SPICED PUMPKIN
½ medium butternut pumpkin (squash), skin left on, cut in half and seeds removed
3 tablespoons extra virgin olive oil
3 tablespoons ras el hanout (a North African spice blend)
400 g (14 oz) ricotta cheese

HARISSA YOGHURT
300 g (10½ oz) Greek-style yoghurt
30 g (1 oz) harissa paste
3 teaspoons lime juice

FOR THE PUMPKIN Preheat the oven to 180°C (350°F).

Coat the pumpkin with the olive oil and ras el hanout and season with salt and pepper. Cover each half with foil and bake for 1¼ hours, or until tender. Remove from the oven and leave to cool.

Scoop out the flesh, discarding the skin. Warm the pumpkin in a saucepan over low heat, then stir in the ricotta and cook until the mixture is hot. Keep warm.

FOR THE HARISSA YOGHURT Combine all the ingredients and set aside.

TO POACH THE EGGS Fill a wide saucepan with about 8 cm (3¼ inches) of water. Add the vinegar and salt and bring to the boil. Reduce the heat to medium–low, so the water is just simmering, with small bubbles rising from the bottom of the pan and small ripples across the top of the water.

Using a wooden spoon or whisk, stir the simmering water in one direction to create a whirlpool; this will help give your poached eggs a neat shape.

Crack an egg into a saucer. Slide the egg from the saucer as close to the water as possible, into the centre of the whirlpool. Cook, without stirring, for 2–3 minutes for a semi-soft yolk, or 3–4 minutes for a firm-set yolk.

Using a slotted spoon, transfer the egg to paper towel to drain. Season and keep warm while cooking the remaining eggs, one at a time.

TO SERVE Place the toasts on serving plates and spread with a generous spoonful of the pumpkin mash. Top with the poached eggs, then a good dollop of the harissa yoghurt. Sprinkle with the dukkah, chives, thyme leaves, and finish with a drizzle of olive oil.

You can add all sorts of different ingredients to a good frittata recipe base, and it's a great way to use up those forgotten vegetables lurking in the fridge. If celeriac isn't in season, use potato or parsnip instead. You'll find the Spanish hams jamón iberico and jamón de bellota in delicatessens, but if you can't get hold of any, opt for a good country-style prosciutto. The corn salsa is also great alongside fresh prawns or barbecued chicken.

Celeriac & chorizo frittata with jamón & corn salsa

MAKES 10 SMALL PIECES

FOR THE CORN SALSA Cook the corn in a saucepan of salted boiling water for 5 minutes. Refresh in ice-cold water, then drain and pat dry. Cut the kernels off the husk and place in a bowl. Add the remaining ingredients and mix well. Season with salt and pepper.

FOR THE FRITTATA Preheat the oven to 180°C (350°F). Grease and line an 18 x 28 cm (7 x 11¼ inch) slab tin (or similar shallow baking tin) with baking paper.

Peel the celeriac, cut it in half, then cut into 1.5 cm (⅝ inch) dice. Place on the baking tray, drizzle with olive oil, season well, then bake for 10–15 minutes, or until just cooked.

Heat a non–stick frying pan over medium heat. Add the onion and another drizzle of olive oil and cook for 3–4 minutes, or until the onion is just tender. Add the chorizo and rosemary and cook, stirring, for 4–5 minutes. Add the celeriac and cook for another 2–3 minutes. Season to taste.

Crack the eggs into a bowl, add the milk and mix with a fork to combine. Spoon the celeriac and chorizo mixture into the lined tin, spreading it evenly over the base. Pour the egg mixture over the top and scatter with the goat's cheese.

Bake for 30–35 minutes, or until the frittata is set and the top is golden. Rest for 5 minutes before cutting into 10 portions.

Serve warm, with the jamón and corn salsa.

CORN SALSA
1 corn cob
1 avocado, diced
½ long green chilli (or to taste), finely chopped
50 g (1¾ oz) French shallots, finely diced
1 teaspoon smoked paprika
30 g (1 oz) flat-leaf (Italian) parsley, roughly chopped
¼ bunch coriander (cilantro), leaves only, roughly chopped
juice of ½ lemon
3 tablespoons extra virgin olive oil

FOR THE FRITTATA
400 g (14 oz) celeriac
extra virgin olive oil, for drizzling
1 red onion, finely chopped
240 g (8½ oz) chorizo sausages, roughly chopped; to make your own, see page 152
1 teaspoon rosemary leaves, finely chopped
6 free-range eggs
3 tablespoons milk
60 g (2¼ oz) goat's feta
100 g (3½ oz) jamón iberico or jamón de bellota, chopped or sliced

Chilled chia custards with chopped fruit, pistachios & coconut yoghurt (page 20)

Macadamia & zucchini fritters with smoked salmon & corn salsa (page 30)

Crispy bacon &
egg tacos with
pico de gallo &
kimchi mayo
(page 21)

Smashed spiced
pumpkin & ricotta on rye
with poached eggs
(page 16)

This is surely the ultimate summer power breakfast. Feel free to vary the fruit according to what's in season; just ensure it is nice and ripe.

Chilled chia custards with chopped fruit, pistachios & coconut yoghurt

MAKES 8

170 g (5¾ oz/⅔ cup) thick, good-quality coconut yoghurt

CHIA CUSTARD
500 ml (17 fl oz/2 cups) almond milk
80 g (2¾ oz/½ cup) chia seeds
4 tablespoons maple syrup
¼ vanilla bean, cut in half lengthways, seeds scraped

FRUIT SALAD
80 g (2¾ oz) rockmelon, finely diced
80 g (2¾ oz) honeydew melon, finely diced
8 strawberries, finely diced
8 raspberries, halved
60 g (2¼ oz) blueberries
80 g (2¾ oz) pineapple, finely diced
80 g (2¾ oz) mango, finely diced
1 orange, peeled, segmented and finely diced
80 g (2¾ oz) watermelon, cut into 1 cm (½ inch) pieces
2 teaspoons lime juice
2 tablespoons pistachio nuts, toasted, peeled and roughly chopped
8 large mint leaves

FOR THE CHIA CUSTARD Heat the almond milk in a saucepan over medium heat, to just below boiling point. Remove from the heat and add the chia seeds, maple syrup, and the vanilla pod and seeds, mixing well. Transfer to a bowl, cover and refrigerate for 1 hour.
Mix again, then refrigerate overnight.

FOR THE FRUIT SALAD Near serving time, combine all the fruit in a mixing bowl. Add the lime juice and pistachios. Tear or slice the mint leaves and add most of them to the fruit salad, reserving some as a garnish. Mix well.

TO SERVE Spoon the chia custard mixture into eight small glasses or serving bowls. Top each one with the fruit salad and a dollop of coconut yoghurt. Serve garnished with the reserved mint.

If you are time poor, you can buy good-quality kimchi from Asian supermarkets instead of making your own. Kewpie mayo is the most popular mayonnaise in Japan and has a beautiful flavour; you will find it in most good supermarkets these days.

Crispy bacon & egg tacos with pico de gallo & kimchi mayo

MAKES 8 TACOS

FOR THE PICO DE GALLO Near serving time, finely chop the tomatoes, shallots and chilli, adjusting the amount of jalapeño to your taste; for a spicier pico, leave the seeds in. Place in a bowl. Add the coriander, mint, cumin, lime juice and olive oil. Stir to combine, season with salt and pepper, then add Tabasco to taste.

FOR THE KIMCHI MAYO Just before serving, combine the kimchi and mayonnaise in a bowl.

TO SERVE Heat a large non-stick frying pan over medium–high heat. Spray the pan with oil and cook the bacon for a few minutes on each side, until lightly golden. Transfer to a plate and cover with foil to keep warm.

Pan-fry the eggs, keeping them a little runny, and transfer to a plate.

Wipe out the pan and reduce the heat to medium. Warm the tortillas for a few seconds on each side, then place on a board and fill each one with the lettuce, bacon, eggs and pico de gallo.

Top with the kimchi mayo, garnish with the coriander and serve.

cooking oil spray
8 middle bacon rashers, rind removed, cut in half
8 free-range eggs
8 small tortillas
¼ small iceberg lettuce, thinly sliced
¼ bunch coriander (cilantro), leaves picked

PICO DE GALLO
2–3 roma (plum) tomatoes
2 French shallots
1 jalapeño chilli, chopped
¼ bunch coriander (cilantro), leaves only, chopped
¼ bunch mint, leaves only, chopped
½ teaspoon cumin seeds, toasted and ground
juice of 1 lime
70 ml (2¼ fl oz) extra virgin olive oil
Tabasco or other hot sauce, to taste

KIMCHI MAYO
½ cup Cabbage kimchi (page 225), roughly chopped
125 g (4 oz/½ cup) kewpie mayonnaise

Here's how to put the glamour on the classic ham and cheese toasted sandwich — but you really do need to use good smoked ham and gruyère cheese. This recipe can easily be doubled to feed a larger crowd.

Smoked ham, tomato, creamed chard & gruyère toasties

MAKES 4

FOR THE CREAMED CHARD Melt the butter in a saucepan over medium heat. Add the shallot and cook for 3 minutes, until translucent. Add the flour and cook, stirring constantly, for 1 minute.

Add the milk and nutmeg, increase the heat to high and cook, stirring constantly, for 5 minutes, until the mixture has reduced by half.

Add the silverbeet and cook for 3–4 minutes, until it is tender and coated with the thickened milk mixture. Remove from the heat and keep warm.

FOR THE HONEY MUSTARD MAYO Combine all the ingredients and set aside.

TO SERVE Heat up a sandwich press.

On the bottom piece of the Turkish bread, spread a good dollop of the honey mustard mayo, then the creamed chard. Add the ham and the cheese. Spoon the tomato relish over, then sandwich with the top layer of the bread.

Place into the sandwich press and cook until golden brown. Cut into portions to serve.

½ loaf of pide (Turkish bread),
   cut in half widthways
8 slices smoked ham
120 g (4¼ oz) gruyère cheese, sliced
250 g (9 oz/1 cup) Tomato relish
   (page 233)

CREAMED CHARD
2 tablespoons unsalted butter
2–3 French shallots, finely chopped
1 tablespoon plain (all-purpose) flour
250 ml (9 fl oz/1 cup) milk
½ teaspoon ground nutmeg
450 g (1 lb) silverbeet (Swiss chard),
   ribs removed, leaves roughly
   chopped

HONEY MUSTARD MAYO
100 g (3½ oz) mayonnaise
1 tablespoon honey
2 tablespoons wholegrain mustard

Shakshuka is a Middle Eastern breakfast staple. If you don't have time to make the Spinach parathas to enjoy with them, a good loaf of toasted sourdough or Turkish bread will work perfectly.

Shakshuka (eggs baked in tomato sauce) with spinach parathas

SERVES 6

1 tablespoon extra virgin olive oil, plus extra for drizzling

½ onion, finely diced

5 garlic cloves, finely chopped

½ red capsicum (pepper), finely diced

1 red chilli, finely diced

2 teaspoons ground cumin

2 teaspoons sweet paprika

400 g (14 oz) tin crushed tomatoes

6 large free-range eggs

¼ bunch flat-leaf (Italian) parsley, leaves only, chopped

¼ bunch coriander (cilantro), leaves only, chopped

¼ bunch dill, leaves only, chopped

Spinach parathas (page 49), to serve

Heat the olive oil in a frying pan over medium heat. Add the onion and cook for 3–4 minutes, until soft and translucent. Stir in the garlic, capsicum, chilli, cumin and paprika and continue to cook for 2–3 minutes.

Add the tomatoes and reduce the heat to low. Simmer for 10 minutes, until the mixture has thickened slightly. Season to taste.

Meanwhile, preheat the oven to 180°C (350°F).

Place the mixture in an ovenproof dish and onto a baking tray. Use a serving spoon to make six small wells, then crack an egg into each well.

Cover the dish with a plate or foil. Transfer the tray to the oven and bake for 10–12 minutes, until the eggs are just set.

TO SERVE Carefully remove the lid from the dish. Sprinkle with the parsley, coriander and dill. Drizzle with a little extra olive oil and serve warm, with spinach parathas.

I wasn't sure whether to put this recipe in the Breakfast chapter or in Desserts, so I'll let you decide where they belong. Doughnuts would have to be one of my favourite desserts — but they also make a decadent weekend breakfast treat! These ones are beautiful served warm. You can either roll them in cinnamon sugar, or fill them with custard or jam — again, you decide... When in season, try to use fresh rhubarb here, rather than frozen. The jam uses pectin, which you'll find in good supermarkets and fine food stores.

Doughnuts with custard & jam filling

MAKES 12 SMALL DOUGHNUTS

CUSTARD
250 ml (9 fl oz/1 cup) milk
2 teaspoons unsalted butter
100 g (3½ oz) caster (superfine) sugar
1 vanilla bean, cut in half lengthways,
    seeds scraped
45 g (1½ oz) egg yolks (2–3 egg yolks)
1 tablespoon plus 1 teaspoon custard
    powder
1 teaspoon plain (all-purpose) flour

RHUBARB & VANILLA JAM
250 g (9 oz) rhubarb, chopped into small
    pieces and frozen
2 vanilla beans, cut in half lengthways,
    seeds scraped
250 g (9 oz) caster (superfine) sugar
1 tablespoon apple pectin (or any
    good-quality pectin)

CINNAMON SUGAR
1 vanilla bean, cut in half lengthways,
    seeds scraped
2 teaspoons ground cinnamon
200 g (7 oz) caster (superfine) sugar

DOUGHNUTS
265 (9¼ oz/1¾ cups) plain (all-purpose) flour
40 g (1½ oz) caster (superfine) sugar
2 teaspoons dried yeast
1¾ teaspoons sea salt
160 g (5¾ oz) lightly beaten free-range eggs
    (about 3–4 eggs)
125 ml (4 fl oz/½ cup) milk
40 g (1½ oz) unsalted butter
vegetable oil, for deep-frying

FOR THE CUSTARD Combine the milk, butter and 50 g (1¾ oz) of the sugar in a saucepan. Add the scraped vanilla pod and seeds, place over medium heat and bring to boiling point.

In a bowl, combine the egg yolks and remaining sugar and whisk until combined. Add the custard powder and the flour and whisk until the mixture is thick.

Pour half the hot milk mixture over the egg yolk mixture, whisking well.

Pour the egg mixture into a clean saucepan. Add the rest of the hot milk, whisking until it comes back to the boil. Pour into a bowl and cover the surface with plastic wrap to prevent a skin forming. Chill in the fridge for 2 hours.

FOR THE JAM Place all the ingredients in a saucepan with 150 ml (5 fl oz) water. Simmer over low heat until the rhubarb begins to soften. Cook for 30 minutes, or until the mixture has a jam-like consistency. Set aside to cool.

FOR THE CINNAMON SUGAR Simply combine all the ingredients in a shallow bowl.

FOR THE DOUGHNUTS Fit a dough hook attachment to an electric stand mixer. Place the flour, sugar, yeast and salt into the mixer bowl. Set the mixer to its lowest speed. Slowly add the eggs and milk. Mix for 15 minutes, or until the mixture becomes very smooth and begins to form a ball shape. Add the butter and continue mixing until the dough is smooth and shiny, and leaves the side of the bowl easily; it should be quite elastic. Cover the dough with plastic wrap and refrigerate for a minimum of 2 hours.

Weigh the dough into twelve 15–17 g (½ oz) portions and roll into balls.

Two-thirds fill a deep-fryer or large heavy-based saucepan with vegetable oil. Heat to 180°C (350°F), or until a cube of bread dropped into the oil turns golden brown in 15 seconds.

Add the doughnuts in batches and cook until golden brown, about 4–5 minutes, turning regularly. Drain on paper towels and leave to cool.

TO SERVE If using the jam or custard, place in a piping (icing) bag. Pierce a small hole in the side of the doughnuts and pipe the jam or custard.

Alternatively, roll the warm doughnuts in the cinnamon sugar.

I loved jaffles as a kid. And I still do. Instead of kale, you can use silverbeet (Swiss chard) in these ones, although kale is widely available these days and less expensive than it once was. Jaffles are also perfect for using up leftovers.

Curried kale, sweet potato, caramelised onion & mozzarella jaffles

MAKES 4 WHOLE OR 8 HALF JAFFLES

FOR THE FILLING Heat 3 tablespoons of the olive oil in a heavy-based saucepan over medium heat, until the oil is shimmering. Add the onion and cook, stirring frequently, for 5 minutes, or until softened. Add the sweet potato, cover the pan and cook, stirring occasionally, for 5 minutes, until the sweet potato is bright orange. Transfer to a bowl and set aside.

Increase the heat to medium–high and add the remaining oil to the pan. Add the garlic, ginger, chilli flakes and curry powder and cook, stirring constantly, for 30 seconds, until fragrant.

Add half the kale and stir for 1 minute, until it begins to wilt, then add the remaining kale, along with the stock, coconut milk and salt. Put the lid on and reduce the heat to low. Cook, stirring occasionally, until the kale has wilted; this will take 8–10 minutes.

Now stir in the sweet potato mixture. Cover and cook for another 8–10 minutes, until the kale and sweet potato are tender. Remove the lid, increase the heat to medium–high. Cook, stirring occasionally, for 3–4 minutes, until most of the liquid has evaporated and the sauce has thickened.

Remove from the heat, Stir in the lime juice and season with salt and pepper. Set aside to cool.

TO SERVE Heat a jaffle maker or sandwich maker.

Spread the onion confit over four slices of the bread. Top with the curried kale and sweet potato mixture, spreading it evenly, then add three slices of the mozzarella. Top with the remaining bread slices to make a sandwich.

Cook in a jaffle maker until golden brown. Enjoy hot.

Onion confit (page 230), for
    spreading
8 slices white bread
4 buffalo mozzarella balls, each
    cut into 3 slices

CURRIED KALE & SWEET POTATO FILLING
100 ml (3½ fl oz) extra virgin olive oil
1 onion, finely chopped
900 g (2 lb) orange sweet potato,
    peeled and cut into 1 cm (½ inch)
    cubes
5 garlic cloves, crushed
2 cm (¾ inch) piece of fresh ginger,
    peeled and grated
½ teaspoon chilli flakes
2 tablespoons curry powder
800 g (1 lb 12 oz) kale, washed,
    coarse stalks removed, leaves
    chopped
250 ml (9 fl oz/1 cup) vegetable stock
100 ml (3½ fl oz) coconut milk
½ teaspoon sea salt
80 ml (2½ fl oz/⅓ cup) lime juice

These fritters make a lovely brunch. We deep-fry ours, but you could also just shallow-fry them in a frying pan on the stove.

Macadamia & zucchini fritters with smoked salmon & corn salsa

MAKES 8

4 Crumpets (page 40)
olive oil, for pan-frying
150 g (5½ oz) baby English spinach leaves
400 g (14 oz) smoked salmon
8 warm poached eggs (see page 16)
60 g (2¼ oz) piece of fresh horseradish, peeled

CORN SALSA
1 cooked corn cob, kernels removed
1 avocado, flesh diced
⅛ red onion, finely diced
½ red chilli, chopped
¼ bunch Vietnamese mint, leaves only, roughly chopped
¼ bunch coriander (cilantro), leaves only, roughly chopped
2 tablespoons lime juice
2 tablespoons extra virgin olive oil

MACADAMIA & ZUCCHINI FRITTERS
olive oil, for pan-frying
¼ onion, diced
2 garlic cloves, finely chopped
2 teaspoons smoked paprika
2 large zucchini (courgettes)
2 free-range eggs
100 g (3½ oz/⅔ cup) self-raising flour
½ teaspoon baking powder
3 tablespoons macadamia nuts, roughly chopped
vegetable oil, for deep-frying

FOR THE CORN SALSA Just before serving, combine all the ingredients in a bowl, being careful not to break up the avocado too much. Cover and set aside.

FOR THE FRITTERS Heat a drizzle of olive oil in a saucepan over medium heat. Add the onion and garlic and cook for 3–4 minutes, until the onion is softened but not coloured. Add the paprika and cook for 30 seconds, then transfer to a bowl to cool.

Grate the zucchini. Squeeze the zucchini with your hands to remove the excess liquid and set aside.

Whisk the eggs in a bowl. Add the flour, baking powder and a pinch of salt and mix to combine; the mixture should be quite thick. If it is too runny, you will not be able to make fritters, so add a little extra flour. Stir in the grated zucchini and the sautéed onion mixture, then fold in the nuts.

Two-thirds fill a deep-fryer or large heavy-based saucepan with vegetable oil. Heat to 170°C (325°F), or until a cube of bread dropped into the oil turns golden brown in 20 seconds. Using a tablespoon, and working in batches, gently place dollops of the fritter mixture into the hot oil and cook for 3–4 minutes, turning a few times. Drain on paper towel and season with salt and pepper.

TO SERVE Toast the crumpets in a toaster until golden.

Heat a drizzle of olive oil in a frying pan over medium heat, then cook the spinach for 1–2 minutes, until wilted. Season, then transfer to paper towels and squeeze out as much liquid as possible.

Place the toasted crumpets on serving plates. Top each with a little spinach, smoked salmon, a poached egg and a dollop of corn salsa. Grate the horseradish over the top. Season again and serve with the warm zucchini fritters.

I love baking this bread on cold winter days, when the smell of baked apple seems to warm the whole house. The ricotta gives this dish a great balance of sweet and savoury.

Toasted apple & walnut bread with ricotta, smashed banana & fresh honeycomb

SERVES 6–8

2 bananas
165 g (5¾ oz/⅔ cup) ricotta cheese
175 g (6 oz/½ cup) honey from fresh honeycomb
16 walnut halves, toasted and roughly chopped

APPLE & WALNUT BREAD
40 g (1½ oz/¼ cup) grated carrot
185 g (6½ oz/¾ cup) apple sauce
3 tablespoons vegetable oil
½ teaspoon vanilla essence
1 free-range egg
75 g (2½ oz/⅓ cup) soft brown sugar
70 g (2½ oz) butter, melted
100 ml (3½ fl oz) milk
35 g (1¼ oz/¼ cup) walnut pieces
165 g (5¾ oz) self-raising flour
¼ teaspoon sea salt
½ teaspoon baking powder
¼ teaspoon bicarbonate of soda (baking soda)
¾ teaspoon ground cinnamon
¼ teaspoon ground nutmeg

FOR THE BREAD Preheat the oven to 175°C (330°F). Grease and line an 11 x 26 cm (4¼ x 10½ inch) loaf (bar) tin.

In a mixing bowl, combine the carrot, apple sauce, vegetable oil and vanilla. Add the egg and sugar and mix together. Add the melted butter and milk and mix to combine.

In another bowl, mix together the walnuts and remaining dry ingredients. Add them to the carrot mixture and stir to combine, but do not over-mix.

Spoon the mixture into the loaf tin. Bake for 55 minutes, or until the bread springs back when gently pressed.

Remove from the oven and cool in the tin for 10 minutes, before turning out onto a wire rack to cool for 20 minutes.

TO SERVE Heat the grill (broiler) to high. Peel the bananas, place in a bowl and crush with a fork.

Slice the cooled apple and walnut bread and toast on both sides under the grill.

Serve warm, topped with a spoonful of the ricotta, the mashed banana, a drizzle of honey and the chopped walnut pieces.

Feuilletine (pronounced foo-yee-teen) are sweet, buttery, crispy crumbs that add a delicious crunch to creamy desserts. You can buy feuilletine from good bakeries or fine food stores, or simply use corn flakes to give the granola the same crunch.

Roasted nut & quinoa granola with coconut, honey & berries

SERVES 4

FOR THE TOASTED GRANOLA Preheat the oven to 160°C (315°F).

Spread the nuts, oats and coconut on a baking tray. Bake for 10–15 minutes, until golden, lightly mixing the granola throughout the cooking process. Leave to cool, then tip onto a chopping board and roughly chop.

Increase the oven temperature to 170°C (325°F).

Return the nut and oat mixture to the tray. Add the remaining granola ingredients and mix to combine. Bake for 5–10 minutes, until a nice golden colour.

TO SERVE Place the toasted granola in serving dishes and top with the strawberries, blueberries and coconut. Add a good dollop of the yoghurt, drizzle with warm honey and garnish with the mint leaves. Serve with soy milk on the side.

125 g (4½ oz) strawberries, hulled and quartered
60 g (2¼ oz) blueberries
50 g (1¾ oz) desiccated (shredded) coconut, toasted
125 g (4¼ oz/½ cup) organic plain yoghurt
warmed honey, for drizzling
8 mint leaves, torn if large
soy milk, to serve

TOASTED GRANOLA
20 g (¾ oz) pistachio nuts
75 g (2½ oz) slivered almonds
45 g (1½ oz/⅓ cup) walnuts
125 g (4½ oz) rolled (porridge) oats
35 g (1¼ oz) desiccated coconut
30 g (1 oz) cooked quinoa
30 g (1 oz) pepitas (pumpkin seeds)
50 g (1¾ oz) brown sugar
75 g (2½ oz) honey
3 teaspoons extra virgin olive oil
1 teaspoon vanilla essence
125 g (4½ oz) feuilletine

When it comes to eggs, always buy the freshest free-range ones you can find as you really will taste the difference. Truffle salt is stocked by good grocers and fine food stores. You can substitute the asparagus, when not in season, with broccolini.

Soft-boiled eggs with asparagus, truffle salt & sourdough soldiers

SERVES 4

4 free-range eggs, at room temperature
2 slices sourdough bread
80 g (2¾ oz) unsalted butter
½ teaspoon truffle salt
4 asparagus spears, cut in half, blanched and refreshed in iced water

Place the eggs in a small saucepan and cover with cold water. Put the lid on and bring to the boil over high heat, then reduce the heat to medium. Simmer gently for 2 minutes, then remove from the heat.

Meanwhile, toast the bread in a toaster until golden. Cut the crusts off, then cut the bread into large batons and spread with butter.

Use a slotted spoon to remove the eggs from the water and transfer to egg cups. Using a knife, carefully remove the tops from eggs (about one-third of the way down). Season with the truffle salt and serve with the sourdough soldiers and asparagus spears.

This is a lovely special-occasion brunch with a glass of champagne.

Toasted crumpets with salmon gravlax, feta, cucumber & horseradish

FOR THE SALMON Place the salmon on a flat tray. In a bowl, combine the rock salt and sugar. Pour the Cognac over the salmon and rub it into the flesh. Smear both sides of the salmon with the salt and sugar mixture. Cover with plastic wrap, then place in the fridge for 2 hours to cure.

Rinse the salmon with water, then pat dry with paper towel. Place on a clean tray, skin side down, and drizzle with olive oil. Scatter the chopped dill over the fish, pressing it on with your fingers.

Using a very sharp knife, slice the salmon very thinly. Place on a tray, ready for serving.

TO SERVE Toast the crumpets and place on a tray. Top with the salmon slices. Combine the rocket and cucumber in a bowl and place on the salmon. Crumble the feta over the top.

Combine the crème fraîche with the lemon juice, then drizzle over the crumpets. Top with the grated horseradish and a sprinkling of cracked black pepper and serve.

8 Crumpets (page 40), cut in half
handful baby rocket (arugula) leaves
1 Lebanese (short) cucumber,
    cut into ribbons
80 g (2¾ oz) Persian feta
60 g (2¼ oz) crème fraîche
juice of ½ lemon
40 g (1½ oz) piece of fresh
    horseradish, peeled and grated

SALMON GRAVLAX
600 g (1 lb 5 oz) salmon fillet, skin
    and bones removed
160 g (5¾ oz/½ cup) rock salt
110 g (3¾ oz/½ cup) soft brown sugar
2½ tablespoons Cognac
extra virgin olive oil, for drizzling
½ bunch dill, leaves finely chopped

Chapter 2
Bread

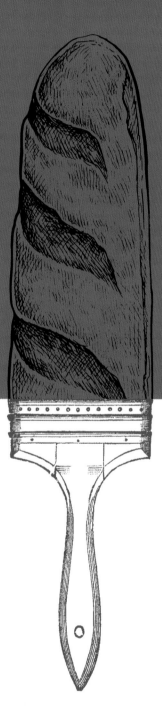

Baking bread is one of life's greatest little pleasures. There's something very satisfying about taking the time to make your own, and sharing it with friends.

When I was a kid, Mum had to find a way to fill up the stomachs of seven hungry sons, so there was often a loaf of bread baking in the oven. The smell that filled our busy house was pure comfort.

For me, bread isn't just something you have on the side to fill the table: it can be a meal in itself. During one of my first trips to Paris, I didn't have enough money to eat at all the fancy places, so I lived on warm baguettes and fresh butter — just delicious!

Baking your own bread isn't at all difficult; it just requires a bit of forward planning to allow time for your batter to rest or your dough to rise. For this chapter, I've put together some of my favourites, including a simple but really delicious English muffin (page 54); a warm focaccia three ways (page 50), which pairs well with the meatballs on page 165; and a slightly more challenging spinach paratha (page 49) to accompany Indian-style dishes such as the Chicken garam masala on page 174.

I hope these wonderful recipes bring you many hours of baking enjoyment, sharing the pleasure of breaking bread with family and friends.

Here's a great crumpet recipe to have up your sleeve. Beautiful toasted with any type of topping, sweet or savoury, these taste nothing like the store-bought variety. Even better, any leftover crumpets can be frozen.

Crumpets

MAKES 18 SMALL CRUMPETS

185 ml (6 fl oz/¾ cup) milk
1 teaspoon dried yeast
½ teaspoon caster (superfine) sugar
185 g (6½ oz) plain (all-purpose) flour
¼ teaspoon bicarbonate of soda
    (baking soda)
pinch of sea salt
olive oil, for brushing

FOR THE CRUMPETS In a saucepan, warm the milk to body temperature over medium heat. Remove from the heat, making sure the milk is not too hot, or you will kill the yeast. Stir in the yeast and sugar. Stand for 10 minutes, or until mixture starts bubbling.

Sift the flour, bicarbonate of soda and salt into a mixing bowl and make a well in the centre. Using an electric mixer, gradually beat in the milk mixture and 90 ml (3 fl oz) water until you have a very smooth batter.

Cover with plastic wrap and stand in a warm place for 1–1½ hours, or until the mixture has doubled in size.

Heat a frying pan over low heat for 1–2 minutes. Dig out some 6 cm (2½ inch) crumpet rings, about 3 cm (1¼ inches) deep, and grease them. Place in the pan and add 2 tablespoons of batter to each. Cook over low heat for 5 minutes, or until the surface is full of large bubbles and a skin has formed. Loosen the rings and remove. Carefully turn the crumpets over and cook for a further few minutes. Transfer to a wire rack to cool.

Continue making the crumpets, until all the batter has been used.

TO SERVE Toast the crumpets until golden brown, either in a toaster, or under a hot grill (broiler). Serve hot, with butter, fresh honey, or your favourite topping.

You'll find all the ingredients for the Japanese seaweed butter at good Asian grocers. Don't be afraid to experiment a little — instead of the kombu and wakame you could use lots of soft fresh herbs like basil, chives and chervil. These popovers are best served warm, straight from the oven.

Rosemary popovers with seaweed butter

MAKES 12 POPOVERS

FOR THE SEAWEED BUTTER Place the kombu and wakame in a bowl, with enough warm water just to cover. Allow to soak for 1 hour.

Drain the kombu and wakame and finely slice. Add to a bowl with the remaining ingredients and mix with a spatula.

Place the butter mixture on a sheet of plastic wrap, roll into a sausage and wrap the ends up securely. Refrigerate until required; the butter will last for about 1 week in the fridge, or in the freezer for up to 3 months.

FOR THE ROSEMARY POPOVERS Preheat the oven to 200°C (400°F).

Place the flour in a bowl and beat in the eggs with a wooden spoon until smooth. Gradually add the milk and continue beating until the mixture is completely lump-free. Season with salt and fold in the rosemary leaves. Pour the batter into a jug.

Drizzle a generous amount of sunflower oil into each hole of a standard 12-hole (60 ml/2 fl oz) non-stick muffin tin. Place the muffin tin in the oven for 10 minutes to heat the oil.

Remove the hot muffin tin from the oven and carefully and evenly pour the batter into the holes. Return to the oven and bake for 15–20 minutes, until the batter has puffed up and browned.

Spread with the seaweed butter and serve.

90 g (3¼ oz) plain (all-purpose) flour
3 free-range eggs
150 ml (5 fl oz) milk
4 rosemary sprigs, leaves finely chopped
sunflower oil, for greasing

SEAWEED BUTTER
50 g (1¾ oz) dried kombu seaweed
50 g (1¾ oz) dried wakame seaweed
200 g (7 oz) unsalted butter, softened
1 small French shallot, finely chopped
1 garlic clove, chopped
pinch of sansho pepper
3 tablespoons mirin

Crumpets (page 40)

Rosemary popovers
with seaweed butter
(page 41)

Potato, caramelised onion, fig, gorgonzola & grilled radicchio pizzas (page 46)

Truffled mushroom & pecorino flatbreads (page 44)

Truffle salsa adds some luxury to these simple flatbreads. If you can't find it in fine food stores, just use a little more truffle oil in the truffle topping. These flatbreads pair well with the seared scallops on page 118.

Truffled mushroom & pecorino flatbreads

MAKES 12–15 PIECES

MUSHROOM DUXELLES
2½ tablespoons olive oil
1 kg (2 lb 4 oz) button mushrooms, sliced
5 thyme sprigs
1.5 litres (52 fl oz/6 cups) red wine

FLATBREADS
275 g (9¾ oz) plain (all-purpose) flour
good pinch of sea salt
70 ml (2¼ fl oz) milk
2 teaspoons dried yeast
extra virgin olive oil, for cooking

TRUFFLED MUSHROOM & PECORINO TOPPING
250 g (9 oz) mushroom duxelles (see left)
2 tablespoons truffle salsa
1½ tablespoons truffle oil
150 g (5½ oz/1¾ cups) grated pecorino cheese
150 g (5½ oz/1½ cups) grated parmesan cheese
handful baby rocket (arugula)
extra virgin olive oil, for drizzling

FOR THE MUSHROOM DUXELLES Warm the olive oil in a large saucepan over medium heat. Add the mushrooms and cook, stirring, for about 10 minutes, until there is no liquid remaining.

Stir in the thyme sprigs and wine and continue cooking for a further 10 minutes, until the liquid has reduced to a thick syrup. Remove from the heat to cool slightly.

Discard the thyme sprigs, then transfer to a blender and blitz until roughly chopped. Place in a bowl and allow to cool.

FOR THE TRUFFLED MUSHROOM TOPPING
Once the mushroom duxelles mixture has cooled, add the truffle salsa, truffle oil, 100 g (3½ oz) of the pecorino and 100 g (3½ oz) of the parmesan. Season with salt and pepper and mix to combine. Set aside while making the flatbreads.

FOR THE FLATBREADS Place the flour and salt in a mixing bowl. Warm the milk and 70 ml (2¼ fl oz) water to body temperature, then add the yeast, stirring to combine. Slowly add this to the flour and mix well using your hands for 4–5 minutes, until a dough has formed. Rest the dough for 10–15 minutes in a warm place.

Divide the dough into three even portions. Using a rolling pin, roll out each portion to form rectangles about 5 mm (¼ inch) thick. Allow the dough to prove in a warm place for another 10 minutes.

Preheat a barbecue, chargrill pan or frying pan to medium–hot. Drizzle with a little olive oil. Cook the flatbreads, in batches if necessary, for 2 minutes on each side.

TO SERVE Preheat the oven to 180°C (350°F). Place the flatbreads on baking trays and spread them with the truffled mushroom mix. Sprinkle with the remaining pecorino and parmesan and season to taste.

Bake for 4–5 minutes, or until the cheese has melted. Cut each flatbread into four or five pieces, top with the rocket and drizzle with olive oil. Serve warm.

If you don't have a pizza oven, place the pizza bases on a heavy-based baking tray and cook in your oven at its highest setting until lovely and crisp.

Potato, caramelised onion, fig, gorgonzola & grilled radicchio pizzas

MAKES 2 LARGE PIZZAS

1 head of radicchio
extra virgin olive oil, for drizzling
3 large waxy (boiling) potatoes, such as
    desiree or sebago
6 fresh figs, sliced
140 g (5 oz) gorgonzola cheese, crumbled
8 basil leaves, torn

CARAMELISED ONION
100 g (3½ oz) unsalted butter
2 onions, sliced
100 ml (3½ fl oz) honey
100 ml (3½ fl oz) dry white wine
2½ tablespoons balsamic vinegar

PIZZA DOUGH
250 g (9 oz/1⅔ cups) plain (all-purpose) flour
½ teaspoon sea salt
1 teaspoon dried yeast
extra virgin olive oil, for greasing

FOR THE CARAMELISED ONION Melt the butter in a saucepan over medium heat. When it just starts to froth, add the onion and reduce the heat to low. Cook the onion for about 10 minutes, without colouring. Stir in the honey and wine, mixing well. Continue cooking over a very low heat for 45 minutes.

Add the vinegar and season with salt and pepper to taste. Remove from the heat and cool to room temperature.

FOR THE PIZZA DOUGH Combine the flour and salt in a large bowl. Make a well in the centre.

In a separate bowl, mix the yeast and 125 ml (4 fl oz/½ cup) warm water together with a fork. Add to the flour and mix to form a dough.

Turn out onto a lightly floured bench and knead the dough for 10 minutes, until smooth and elastic. Place in an oiled bowl, cover with plastic wrap or a tea towel, and leave in a warm place to prove for 30 minutes.

TO GRILL THE RADICCHIO Heat a barbecue hotplate or heavy-based frying pan to medium–high.

Cut the radicchio into eight wedges, drizzle with olive oil and season with salt and pepper. Cook for about 3 minutes, turning once, until just tender. Leave to cool.

FOR THE POTATO Thinly slice the potatoes. Place in a steamer and steam for 3 minutes, or until just cooked. Set aside to cool.

TO ASSEMBLE AND COOK THE PIZZA Preheat a pizza oven to 240°C (475°F), or your oven to its highest setting.

Divide the pizza dough into two even portions. Spread each portion of the pizza dough onto its own large, round pizza tray with your fingertips, to form a thin base — the edges don't need to be even.

Place a thin layer of the onion over each, leaving a 2.5 cm (1 inch) rim clear around the edge. Arrange the potatoes on top and season. Add the sliced figs and grilled radicchio. Top with the crumbled gorgonzola.

Bake for 10–15 minutes, until the pizza base is crispy and the top is golden brown. Garnish with the torn basil, drizzle with a little olive oil, cut into wedges and serve hot.

These Indian breads are traditionally cooked on a tava pan — a flat round metal cooking plate with a long handle, also used for cooking roti and other flatbreads. A tava pan doesn't have sides, making it easy to flip the flatbreads during cooking, but you can also use a cast-iron pan. This recipe can be a little tricky first time round, but there are plenty of online videos these days with visual step-by-step instructions to help you. The end result will be worth it.

Spinach parathas

Combine the flour, egg and olive oil in a bowl, mixing well.

Place the spinach, yoghurt, garlic, salt and spices in a blender. Whiz to a smooth paste, adding a little water if necessary, then add to the flour mixture and mix to form a medium-firm dough. You may need to add some water.

Shape the dough into a ball, then rub a few drops of vegetable oil on the top to stop the dough drying out. Cover and rest for 15–20 minutes in a warm place.

Heat a tava pan, cast-iron pan or skillet over medium heat.

Knead the dough on a floured surface for 2–3 minutes. Divide into golf ball sized portions, roughly 80 g (2¾ oz) each. Roll one portion at a time into a smooth ball and flatten it out with your palms on a clean bench. Smear each piece of dough with a little vegetable oil.

Stretch one piece of dough out from the sides until it is four times its original size. Fold back into the centre from all of the corners, to make a round, 13–15 cm (5–6 inch) diameter paratha. Repeat with the remaining dough balls.

One at a time, place a paratha onto the pan and cook over low heat until bubbles appear. Flip it over and cook for 1–2 minutes. Lightly brush more oil on top, then flip it over again and cook for another minute.

Transfer to a plate and cover with a clean towel to keep warm, while cooking the remaining parathas.

The parathas are best served warm. They can be reheated by wrapping in foil and warming in a 180°C (350°F) oven for 5 minutes.

325 g (11½ oz/2¼ cups) plain (all-purpose) flour, plus extra for dusting
1 free-range egg
1 tablespoon extra virgin olive oil
250 g (9 oz) spinach, blanched
3 tablespoons plain yoghurt
2 large garlic cloves, peeled
1 teaspoon sea salt
¼ teaspoon ground turmeric
¼ teaspoon ground cumin
¼ teaspoon chilli powder
vegetable oil, for greasing

Three toppings on the one focaccia: it's a triple treat! The toppings here are a great starting point, but be creative and include your own favourites. Tasty candidates include green olive tapenade, caramelised onion, anchovy strips, sun-dried tomato pesto...

Focaccia three ways

MAKES 1 LARGE LOAF, YIELDING ABOUT 12 GENEROUS PIECES

FOCACCIA DOUGH
600 g (1 lb 5 oz/4 cups) strong white bread
    flour, plus extra for dusting
150 g (5½ oz) fine semolina
2 teaspoons sea salt
3 teaspoons dried yeast
1 teaspoon caster (superfine) sugar
extra virgin olive oil, for greasing

BALSAMIC ONION TOPPING
extra virgin olive oil, for pan-frying
4 red onions, finely sliced
3–4 thyme sprigs, leaves picked
250 ml (9 fl oz/1 cup) balsamic vinegar

BASIL & CHERRY TOMATO TOPPING
2 bunches fresh basil, leaves picked
500 g (1 lb 2 oz) heirloom cherry tomatoes,
    halved
4 garlic cloves, thinly sliced
white wine vinegar, for drizzling
extra virgin olive oil, for drizzling

THREE-CHEESE & ROSEMARY TOPPING
100 g (3½ oz) taleggio cheese
300 g (10½ oz) goat's cheese
100 g (3½ oz) parmesan cheese, grated
3 rosemary sprigs, leaves picked
extra virgin olive oil, for drizzling

TO MAKE THE DOUGH Place the flour, semolina and salt in the large bowl of an electric stand mixer fitted with a dough hook attachment. (If you don't have a large mixer, these next few steps can all be done by hand.)

In a separate bowl, combine the yeast, sugar and 450 ml (16 fl oz) lukewarm water and mix together.

Add the yeast mixture to the flour and mix on low speed until all the ingredients come together; this may take a few minutes.

Increase the speed to medium–high and continue mixing for 5 minutes, until you have a smooth, soft, springy dough.

Transfer the dough to a large lightly oiled bowl. Dust a little extra flour over the top of the dough and cover with a tea towel. Leave to prove in a warm place for 30 minutes, or until it doubles in size. While the dough is rising, prepare the toppings.

FOR THE BALSAMIC ONION TOPPING Heat a drizzle of olive oil in a saucepan over medium–low heat. Add the onion and thyme leaves and cook for 8–10 minutes, until the onion is tender. Add the vinegar and allow to reduce for a few minutes, until it thickens. Transfer to a tray to cool.

FOR THE BASIL & CHERRY TOMATO TOPPING
Roughly chop the basil leaves and place in a bowl with the cherry tomatoes and garlic. Add a good splash each of vinegar and olive oil. Season with salt and pepper and mix together.

TO ASSEMBLE THE FOCACCIA Lightly oil a 20 x 30 cm (8 x 12 inch) baking tray.

On a lightly floured bench, knead the dough for 1 minute. Place the dough on the baking tray, spreading it out so it evenly covers the tray. Use your fingers to make dips and wells on the surface.

Spread the balsamic onion topping over one-third of the focaccia, and the basil and tomato topping over another third.

FOR THE THREE-CHEESE & ROSEMARY TOPPING
Break up the taleggio and goat's cheese and place over the remaining third of the focaccia. Sprinkle with the parmesan and rosemary leaves and season with pepper. Finish with a good drizzle of extra virgin olive oil and a sprinkle of sea salt.

TO BAKE THE FOCACCIA Once you've added all the toppings, leave the focaccia in a warm place to prove for a further 20 minutes, while you preheat the oven to 190°C (375°F).

Bake the focaccia for 20–25 minutes, until golden on top and soft in the middle.

Leave to rest for 5 minutes, before cutting and serving.

Focaccia three ways (page 50)

You might never think to whip up your own muffins, but they're so easy and inexpensive to make at home. Warm toasted English muffins were a breakfast staple in our house — delicious with any kind of topping, sweet or savoury; think homemade jams or some fresh smoked salmon and capers.

English muffins

MAKES 6

300 g (10½ oz/2 cups) plain
   (all-purpose) flour, plus extra
   for dusting
2 teaspoons dried yeast
1 teaspoon sea salt
1 tablespoon caster (superfine) sugar
25 g (1 oz) unsalted butter, melted
3 teaspoons milk powder
semolina or polenta, for dusting

Place the flour in a large mixing bowl. Sprinkle the yeast on one side of the flour, and the salt onto the other side of the flour. Add the sugar, butter, milk powder and 150 ml (5 fl oz) water and mix to form a soft dough.

Turn the mixture out onto a lightly floured surface and knead for 10 minutes, or until the dough is soft, smooth and stretchy.

Dust the work surface again, this time with a mixture of the semolina and flour. Put the dough back on top and roll out to a 2.5 cm (1 inch) thickness.

Lightly dust a baking tray with the semolina. Use a 6 cm (2½ inch) straight-sided cutter to cut out six muffins from the dough. Dust them with flour and evenly space them on a baking tray. Dust a little semolina over the top of the muffins and leave to prove in a warm place for 30 minutes.

Heat a hot plate or a heavy-based frying pan to a very low heat. Cook the muffins on the hot plate for 5–6 minutes, then flip them over and cook for another 5–6 minutes.

Remove from the pan and cool slightly. Serve warm, or toasted.

This traditional fruit bread is really delicious served warm or toasted with lots of butter. If you don't have an electric stand mixer, you can do the mixing by hand; you will just need to increase the mixing times.

Fruit & nut bread

MAKES 1 LARGE LOAF, YIELDING ABOUT 8 GENEROUS SLICES

In a bowl, combine the yeast and 125 ml (4 fl oz/ ½ cup) warm water; set aside for 5 minutes until foamy. In a separate bowl, combine the flours, cinnamon, nutmeg and salt.

Using an electric stand mixer fitted with a paddle attachment, beat the butter and sugar at medium speed for about 2 minutes, until creamy. Beat in the eggs, one at a time, then beat in the yeast mixture. With the machine running on low speed, gradually add the flour mixture until a dough forms.

Remove the paddle attachment and replace it with the dough hook. Mix the dough on low to medium speed for 10 minutes, scraping down the side of the bowl now and then, if necessary.

Add the nuts, raisins and mixed peel and continue to mix for 5 minutes, until the dough is smooth and springs back when you press it with your finger.

Set aside for 1 hour, until the dough has nearly doubled in size.

Butter and flour the inside and outer rim of a 12 x 21 cm (4½ x 8¼ inch) non-stick loaf (bar) tin.

Punch the centre of the dough to deflate it. Place the dough on a lightly floured work surface and knead for 3 minutes. Form into a 10 x 20 cm (4 x 8 inch) rectangle and place in the loaf tin. Set aside in a warm place until the dough rises by at least 5 cm (2 inches).

Preheat the oven to 200°C (400°F) and place an oven rack in the centre of the oven.

Bake the loaf for 30–35 minutes, until golden brown. Remove from the oven and leave to cool in the tin for 10 minutes, then remove from the tin and transfer to a wire rack to cool completely.

The bread will keep in airtight container for up to 2 days, and can also be frozen.

1 tablespoon dried yeast
270 g (9½ oz) strong flour, plus extra for dusting
120 g (4¼ oz) wholemeal (whole-wheat) flour
2 tablespoons ground cinnamon
1 teaspoon ground nutmeg
1 teaspoon sea salt
120 g (4¼ oz) unsalted butter, at room temperature, plus extra for greasing
115 g (4 oz) caster (superfine) sugar
3 free-range eggs
60 g (2¼ oz/½ cup) chopped walnuts
60 g (2¼ oz/½ cup) chopped hazelnuts
130 g (4½ oz/¾ cup) raisins
75 g (2½ oz/½ cup) mixed peel (mixed candied citrus peel)

Chapter 3
Snacks & Salads

This is one of those chapters that includes a little bit of everything, for just about everyone, for just about any occasion.

There's a real focus on seasonality, using good wholesome ingredients such as zucchini flowers (page 70) and a few fancier items such as quinoa, which features in the spiced pumpkin salad on page 66, that in turn makes a lovely accompaniment to the salt cod croquettes on page 108.

As a chef, it's important to use and understand seasonal produce. Cooking and designing menus according to the season allows you to be more creative in the kitchen. For me, this way of cooking probably stemmed from growing up in a household that relied on buying ingredients according to what was cheap and readily available. Don't be afraid to substitute certain vegies in these recipes. For instance, if you don't have pumpkin on hand, sweet potato will work just as well in the samosas with curried pumpkin (page 63).

We've also included a few recipes for those times when you just want a good snack to serve up with a nice cold beer or drinks for friends. Nibbles such as our truffle oil, parmesan and chive popcorn (page 60) or seriously addictive crispy fried chickpeas (page 75) should do the trick.

Beautifully sweet and spicy, these nuts are great on their own, but also make a glamorous garnish to scatter over Persian or Indian rice dishes. Seal them up in clean, nicely shaped jars and you also have some lovely handmade gifts for foodie friends and family.

Sugar & spice cashews

Preheat the oven to 170°C (325°F). Line a baking tray with baking paper.

Combine the sugar, salt and spices in a bowl and set aside.

Beat the egg white until frothy but not stiff, then add the cashews and stir to coat evenly. Sprinkle the sugar mixture over the cashews and toss to coat.

Spread the cashews in a single layer on the baking tray and bake for 30 minutes, stirring occasionally. Remove from the oven and separate the cashews as they cool.

When completely cool, transfer the cashews to a bowl, breaking up any that stick together.

The nuts will keep in an airtight container in the pantry for up to 1 week. If the nuts go stale, spread them on a baking tray and warm them in a 170°C (325°F) oven for about 3–4 minutes.

100 g (3½ oz/½ cup) dark brown sugar
2 teaspoons pink salt
½ teaspoon cayenne pepper
½ teaspoon ground cinnamon
1 teaspoon smoked paprika
3 teaspoons Cajun spice mix
1 free-range egg white, at room temperature
500 g (1 lb 2 oz) cashews

If you can't find white truffle oil, black truffle oil will work just as well in this fabulous savoury bar snack.

Truffle oil, parmesan & chive popcorn

2½ tablespoons canola or
vegetable oil
150 g (5½ oz/⅔ cup) good-quality
popping corn

POPCORN COATING
4 teaspoons white truffle oil
80 g (2¾ oz) parmesan cheese,
finely grated
½ bunch chives, chopped

FOR THE POPCORN Heat the oil in a saucepan over medium–high heat. Add three or four popcorn kernels and cover the pan with the lid.

When the kernels pop, add the remaining kernels in an even layer. Cover and lightly shake the pan. When the kernels begin popping, slightly open the lid to release the steam, so that the popcorn is dry and crispy. Leave the pan for about 20 seconds, then take off the heat and continue to shake lightly until the popping stops.

Transfer the popcorn to a bowl immediately.

FOR THE COATING While the popcorn is still warm, drizzle with the truffle oil and scatter the parmesan and chives over. Season with salt and pepper and serve.

Here's a great way to use up those leftover cooked vegies. Instead of pumpkin you could use potato, sweet potato, peas or even greens.

Samosas of curried pumpkin & feta with mint & lime yoghurt

FOR THE SAMOSA DOUGH In a bowl, mix all the ingredients together with your hands until a dough forms. Cover with plastic wrap and refrigerate for 2 hours. Bring to room temperature before rolling.

FOR THE FILLING Preheat the oven to 180°C (350°F).
Rub the pumpkin flesh with olive oil. Sprinkle with the curry powder, season with salt and pepper and cover with foil. Place on a baking tray and bake for 1½ hours, or until tender. Leave to cool for 30 minutes.
Scoop the pumpkin flesh into a bowl and mash with a spoon. When completely cool, add the feta, peas and coriander. Season with salt and pepper and mix to combine.

FOR THE MINT & LIME YOGHURT Near serving time, place all the ingredients in a bowl and mix to combine. Cover and refrigerate until required.

TO MAKE THE SAMOSAS Divide the dough into eight portions. Roll each portion into a ball, then flatten each into a 10 cm (4 inch) circle. Cut each circle in half, dampen the edges, then form each semi-circle into a cone. Fill the cones with the pumpkin mixture. Dampen the edges and pinch to seal.

TO SERVE Two-thirds fill a deep-fryer or large heavy-based saucepan with vegetable oil. Heat to 180°C (350°F), or until a cube of bread dropped into the oil turns golden brown in 15 seconds. In batches, carefully lower the samosas into the oil and cook for 4–6 minutes, or until golden brown. Drain on paper towel.
Rest for 3–5 minutes and serve warm, with the curry dressing and mint & lime yoghurt.

vegetable oil, for deep-frying
Curry dressing (page 227), to serve

SAMOSA DOUGH
200 g (7 oz) ghee, warmed
1 kg (2 lb 4 oz) plain (all-purpose) flour
6 free-range eggs
400 g (14 oz) plain yoghurt
1 teaspoon chaat masala (an Indian spice mix, available from Asian grocery stores)

CURRIED PUMPKIN & FETA FILLING
1 small butternut pumpkin (squash), cut in half, seeds removed
extra virgin olive oil, for drizzling
2 tablespoons curry powder
200 g (7 oz) feta cheese, crumbled
150 g (5½ oz/1 cup) frozen peas
½ bunch coriander (cilantro), leaves only, roughly chopped

MINT & LIME YOGHURT
300 g (10½ oz) plain yoghurt
juice of 1 lime
small handful mint leaves, roughly chopped

A perfect side for any meat dish, these fries are absolutely moreish just on their own. Before cooking them, you first soak the sweet potato chips overnight to remove the starch, then freeze them so they don't fall apart in the deep fryer.

Sweet potato & chilli salt fries with gorgonzola cream

SERVES 4 AS A SIDE OR SNACK

2 medium-sized sweet potatoes
vegetable oil, for deep-frying
30 g (1 oz/¼ cup) cornflour
    (cornstarch)
1 teaspoon chilli salt (see below)

CHILLI SALT
10–12 dried red chillies
1 tablespoon caster (superfine) sugar
100 g (3½ oz) sea salt

GORGONZOLA CREAM
1 tablespoon unsalted butter
1 French shallot, finely chopped
250 ml (9 fl oz/1 cup) pouring (single)
    cream
450 g (1 lb) gorgonzola cheese

FOR THE SWEET POTATOES Cut the sweet potatoes into chips and soak in water overnight.

Two-thirds fill a deep-fryer or large heavy-based saucepan with vegetable oil. Heat to 140°C (275°F), or until a cube of bread dropped into the oil turns golden brown in 35 seconds.

Line a baking tray with baking paper. Drain the chips and dry with paper towel. Place the cornflour in a large bowl or bag, add the chips and shake or toss to coat them in the cornflour.

Working in batches if necessary, fry the chips for 4–6 minutes, or until just cooked. Tip them onto the baking tray and place in the freezer for 20 minutes.

FOR THE CHILLI SALT Blitz the chillies in a food processor for 1 minute, until crumbly and flaky. Add the sugar and salt and continue to process until fine. You'll end up with more chilli salt than you'll need for this recipe, so transfer the remainder to a small airtight container and store in the pantry to use in other dishes.

FOR THE GORGONZOLA CREAM Melt the butter in a pan over medium heat. Cook the shallot for 2–3 minutes, until tender. Stir in the cream and cook for 5–10 minutes, until reduced by half. Reduce the heat to low, add the gorgonzola and stir until it melts. Season to taste.

TO SERVE Reheat the oil in a deep-fryer or heavy-based saucepan to 180°C (350°F), or until a cube of bread dropped into the oil turns golden brown in 15 seconds.

Deep-fry the frozen chips for 3–5 minutes, until crispy. Drain on paper towel and serve hot, sprinkled with the chilli salt, with a bowl of gorgonzola cream.

Quinoa adds a nutty flavour to this decadent warm winter salad, and plays really well with pumpkin. If you can't get hold of stilton, do try to use a good-quality blue cheese in this recipe for a punch of flavour.

Salad of roasted pumpkin, chorizo, chickpeas, quinoa & blue cheese

SERVES 4–6

400 g (14 oz) butternut pumpkin (squash), peeled and cut into 2.5 cm (1 inch) cubes

2 tablespoons Moroccan spice mix

70 ml (2¼ fl oz) extra virgin olive oil, plus 3 tablespoons extra

2 chorizo sausages, skin removed and sliced; to make your own, see page 152

100 g (3½ oz) roasted red capsicum (pepper), sliced

150 g (5½ oz/¾ cup) quinoa, rinsed and drained

100 g (3½ oz) tinned chickpeas, rinsed and drained

1 tablespoon preserved lemon rind, finely chopped

45 g (1½ oz) toasted walnuts, roughly chopped

½ bunch coriander (cilantro), leaves only

¼ bunch flat-leaf (Italian) parsley, leaves only

80 ml (2½ fl oz/⅓ cup) Cabernet sauvignon dressing (page 226)

125 g (4½ oz) stilton cheese

Preheat the oven to 220°C (425°F). Line two baking trays with baking paper.

Put the pumpkin in a large bowl with the Moroccan spice mix. Drizzle with the 70 ml (2¼ oz) olive oil and mix, ensuring the pumpkin is well coated in the oil. Season with salt and pepper. Transfer to one of the baking trays and bake for 15 minutes, or until golden and tender, turning halfway through cooking. Remove from the oven and keep warm.

Turn the oven down to 180°C (350°F). Arrange the chorizo and capsicum slices on the other baking tray and bake for 10 minutes.

Meanwhile, place the quinoa and 375 ml (13 fl oz/ 1½ cups) cold water in a saucepan, cover and bring to the boil over high heat. Reduce the heat to low and simmer for 10–12 minutes, or until all the water has been absorbed.

TO ASSEMBLE Place the warm pumpkin, chorizo and capsicum in a bowl. Add the quinoa, chickpeas, preserved lemon, walnuts, coriander and parsley. Drizzle with the cabernet sauvignon dressing and 2½ tablespoons of the extra olive oil. Season and toss gently to combine.

TO SERVE Transfer the warm salad to a serving dish. Crumble the stilton over the top, drizzle with the remaining extra virgin olive oil and serve.

Take the time to source panko crumbs, as they will give these parsnips a really good crispy texture. This is a beautiful side dish for roast beef and gravy.

Crumbed parsnip with remoulade sauce

Place the parsnips in a saucepan over high heat with enough cold water to cover them. Bring to the boil, then reduce the heat and simmer for 10–15 minutes, or until the parsnips are tender — a knife should go in with a little resistance. Drain and place on a tray. Cool in the fridge.

FOR THE REMOULADE SAUCE Place all the ingredients in a bowl and mix together. Season with salt and pepper and set aside.

TO CRUMB THE PARSNIPS Combine the panko crumbs, parmesan and paprika in a large bowl. In another bowl whisk the eggs with the milk. Place the flour in a third bowl.

Dry the parsnips with paper towel. Dust them with the flour, then dip in the egg and then the crumb mix, coating evenly.

Two-thirds fill a deep-fryer or large heavy-based saucepan with vegetable oil. Heat to 180°C (350°F), or until a cube of bread dropped into the oil turns golden brown in 15 seconds.

Working in batches, deep-fry the parsnips for 3–4 minutes, until golden all over. Drain on paper towel.

Season the hot parsnips with salt and pepper and serve with the remoulade sauce.

4–6 small parsnips, peeled and quartered lengthways

REMOULADE SAUCE
2 tablespoons crème fraîche
2 tablespoons sour cream
1 tablespoon capers, roughly chopped
2 teaspoons dijon mustard
1 tablespoon finely chopped parsley
1 tablespoon finely chopped tarragon
juice of ½ lemon

PARMESAN & PAPRIKA PANKO CRUMBS
100 g (3½ oz) panko crumbs
80 g (2¾ oz) parmesan cheese, freshly grated
2 teaspoons smoked paprika
2 large free-range eggs
125 ml (4 fl oz/½ cup) milk
50 g (1¾ oz/⅓ cup) plain (all-purpose) flour
vegetable oil, for deep-frying

DIY guacamole
(page 71)

Crumbed parsnip with
remoulade sauce (page 67)

Crisp zucchini flowers with goat's cheese & salsa verde (page 70)

Salad of roasted pumpkin, chorizo, chickpeas, quinoa & blue cheese (page 66)

*No wonder this is one of our most popular and longest-serving dishes —
zucchini flowers look so beautiful on a plate! Serve with a crisp glass of
chardonnay, all through spring and summer.*

Crisp zucchini flowers with goat's cheese & salsa verde

MAKES 8

8 zucchini (courgette) flowers
rice flour, for dusting
1 quantity Tempura batter (page 232)
½ punnet mustard cress
vegetable oil, for deep-frying

SALSA VERDE
100 ml (3½ fl oz) port
1 tablespoon sultanas (golden
    raisins)
200 ml (7 fl oz) extra virgin olive oil
1 garlic clove, peeled
½ red bird's eye chilli, chopped
2 anchovies
1 tablespoon dijon mustard
1 tablespoon capers
75 g (2½ oz) flat-leaf (Italian) parsley
75 g (2½ oz) mint leaves
75 g (2½ oz) basil leaves
1 tablespoon lemon juice
2 teaspoons good-quality cabernet
    sauvignon vinegar

GOAT'S CHEESE STUFFING
1 corn cob, husk removed
200 g (7 oz) goat's feta
100 ml (3½ fl oz) pouring (single)
    cream
¼ bunch chives, chopped
3 teaspoons chopped preserved
    lemon rind

FOR THE SALSA VERDE Place the port in a small saucepan and bring to the boil over medium heat. Add the sultanas, remove from the heat and set aside to cool.

Transfer the sultana mixture to a blender. Add the remaining ingredients and 2 tablespoons warm water and blend until smooth.

FOR THE GOAT'S CHEESE STUFFING Cook the corn in a saucepan of salted boiling water for 6–8 minutes, until tender. Refresh in iced water. When cool, cut the kernels off and place in a bowl.

Add the remaining ingredients and mix together. Season with salt and pepper.

TO STUFF THE ZUCCHINI FLOWERS Place the goat's cheese stuffing in a piping (icing) bag. Remove the yellow stamen from the zucchini flowers and pipe the mixture into the zucchini flowers. (Alternatively, you could spoon the stuffing into the flowers.) Enclose the filling tightly inside the petals by twisting the ends gently.

TO SERVE Two-thirds fill a deep-fryer or large heavy-based saucepan with vegetable oil. Heat to 170°C (325°F), or until a cube of bread dropped into the oil turns golden brown in 20 seconds.

Working in batches, lightly coat the zucchini flowers with rice flour, dusting off any excess. Lightly coat the them in the tempura batter, then carefully lower them into the hot oil and cook for 3–4 minutes, until golden. Drain on paper towel and season with salt and pepper.

Drizzle the salsa verde around a serving plate. Top with the warm zucchini flowers, garnish with mustard cress and serve.

This is a really fun, sharing recipe to assemble at the table with your favourite tequila at hand, and can easily be doubled to serve more people. Experiment with the ingredients, adjusting the flavourings to suit your taste.

DIY guacamole

Place the avocado halves on a chopping board. Arrange the chopped tomato, onion, jalapeño slices and coriander leaves in piles around the board.

Pour some olive oil into a jug and place on the board with the lime halves and Tabasco. Now take the whole thing to the table, with some sea salt and a pepper grinder, a bowl of corn chips and an empty bowl for making the guacamole.

TO ASSEMBLE THE GUACAMOLE IN FRONT OF YOUR GUESTS
Scoop the avocado flesh into the bowl. Drizzle with olive oil and squeeze the lime juice over the top. Season the avocado with salt and pepper and mash with a fork.

Add the remaining ingredients and mix well. Serve with corn chips.

1 ripe avocado, cut in half, stone removed
½ vine ripened tomato, chopped
½ red onion, chopped
12 jalapeño chilli slices (from a jar)
½ bunch coriander (cilantro), leaves only, roughly chopped
extra virgin olive oil, for drizzling
1 lime, cut in half
Tabasco or other hot sauce, to taste
corn chips, to serve

For a little more spice, use the Crispy fried chickpeas from page 75 instead of tinned chickpeas. Fabulous with chermoula lamb (page 144) or Moroccan lamb cutlets (page 137), this salad also makes a lovely light vegetarian lunch.

Moroccan cauliflower salad with saffron yoghurt, pine nuts & currants

SERVES 4 AS A SIDE

2 teaspoons Moroccan spice mix
2 tablespoons extra virgin olive oil
½ small cauliflower
150 g (5½ oz) cooked chickpeas
    (drained and rinsed, if using
    tinned)
50 g (1¾ oz/⅓ cup) pine nuts
½ bunch flat-leaf (Italian) parsley,
    leaves only
½ bunch coriander (cilantro),
    leaves only
extra virgin olive oil, for drizzling

PORT-SOAKED CURRANTS
200 ml (7 fl oz) port
55 g (2 oz/⅓ cup) currants

SAFFRON YOGHURT
100 ml (3½ fl oz) warm white wine
1 teaspoon saffron threads
130 g (4¾ oz/½ cup) plain yoghurt
juice of 1 lemon
½ teaspoon dijon mustard
1 tablespoon extra virgin olive oil

FOR THE CAULIFLOWER Preheat the oven to 200°C (400°F). In a small bowl, combine the Moroccan spice mix and olive oil.

Wash and dry the cauliflower, then place on a chopping board, stem down, and cut into 1 cm (½ inch) slices — some will break into little bits, others will stay whole. Place the cauliflower in a large bowl, add the spicy oil mixture and season with salt and pepper. Mix well, using your hands, until everything is well coated.

Tip into a large roasting dish and bake for about 8–10 minutes, or until the cauliflower is tender and crispy. Set aside to cool slightly.

FOR THE SAFFRON YOGHURT Pour the wine into a bowl, add the saffron and leave to infuse for 10 minutes. Add the remaining ingredients and mix to combine, then set aside.

FOR THE PORT-SOAKED CURRANTS Pour the port into a small saucepan and bring to the boil over medium heat. Add the currants, remove from the heat and leave to cool.

TO SERVE Toss the cooled currants in a bowl with the chickpeas, pine nuts, parsley and coriander. Dollop the saffron yoghurt onto a serving plate. Top with the roasted cauliflower, then the chickpea mixture. Drizzle with extra virgin olive oil and serve.

These little morsels are deliciously addictive. I love them tossed through salads, and as a garnish on top of curries.

Crispy fried chickpeas

TO SOFTEN THE CHICKPEAS Place the chickpeas in a large bowl; pick out and discard any stones or debris. Cover the chickpeas with water and discard any that float.

Thoroughly rinse and drain, then place the chickpeas in a large saucepan. Pour in enough cold water to cover by 5–7.5 cm (2–3 inches). Add the bay leaves and salt and bring to the boil over high heat. Reduce the heat, cover and simmer for 1–1½ hours, until softened.

Drain the chickpeas and place on a tray. Refrigerate until cool.

Once cool, place in a bowl and add enough buttermilk to cover. Refrigerate, covered, for 2 hours. Drain off any remaining buttermilk.

TO COOK THE CHICKPEAS Preheat the oven to 90°C (195°F). Line a baking tray with paper towel.

Toss the chickpeas with the arborio rice powder and shake off any excess.

Two-thirds fill a deep-fryer or large heavy-based saucepan with vegetable oil. Heat to 170°C (325°F), or until a cube of bread dropped into the oil turns golden brown in 20 seconds.

Deep-fry the chickpeas in batches for about 3 minutes, until they begin to colour; they should be a very light brown. Remove with a slotted spoon and place on the lined baking tray. Keep warm in the oven.

TO SERVE Prepare the garlic chilli oil by heating the olive oil in a large frying pan over low heat. Add the garlic, chilli, sage leaves and citrus zests and allow to sizzle for 1–2 minutes without colouring.

Add the chickpeas, tossing to coat in the oil. Season with sea salt and serve warm.

300 g (10½ oz) dried chickpeas
3 bay leaves
2 teaspoons sea salt
200 ml (7 fl oz) buttermilk, approximately
55 g (2 oz/¼ cup) arborio rice, ground to a powder using a mortar and pestle or spice grinder
vegetable oil, for deep-frying

GARLIC CHILLI OIL
125 ml (4 fl oz/½ cup) extra virgin olive oil
4 garlic cloves, sliced
½ teaspoon chilli flakes
8 sage leaves
zest of 1 lemon
zest of 1 orange

An icy cold beer or cider is all you need with this enticing little bar snack.

Spicy popcorn

2½ tablespoons canola or
    vegetable oil
150 g (5½ oz/⅔ cup) good-quality
    popping corn

POPCORN COATING
3 free-range egg whites
1 teaspoon ground cumin
1 teaspoon sweet paprika
1 teaspoon cayenne pepper
2 teaspoons curry powder
1 tablespoon brown sugar
2 teaspoons sea salt

FOR THE POPCORN Heat the oil in a saucepan over medium–high heat. Add three or four popcorn kernels and cover the pan with the lid.

When the kernels pop, add the remaining kernels in an even layer. Cover and lightly shake the pan. When the kernels begin popping, slightly open the lid to release the steam, so that the popcorn is dry and crispy. Leave the pan for about 20 seconds, then take off the heat and continue to shake lightly until the popping stops.

Transfer the popcorn to a bowl immediately.

FOR THE COATING Preheat the oven to 100°C (200°F). Line a baking tray with baking paper.

Whisk the egg whites until they become light and fluffy, then fold in the cooked popcorn. Add all the remaining ingredients and mix well.

Transfer the popcorn to the baking tray and bake for 10–15 minutes, until completely dry. Serve warm.

Patatas bravas, or fried potato, is a traditional Spanish tapas dish. Enjoy it on its own, or as part of a shared table spread. It's perfect with the grilled ox tongue on page 143.

Patatas bravas with spicy sauce & garlic aioli

SERVES 4

FOR THE TOMATO SAUCE Place the onion, garlic and olive oil in a saucepan over medium heat. Cook for 3–4 minutes, until the onion has softened. Add the spices and cook, stirring, for 4–5 minutes, then stir in the tomatoes, sugar, vinegar and 80 ml (2½ fl oz/ ⅓ cup) water.

Reduce the heat to low and cook for 30 minutes, stirring occasionally so the mixture doesn't burn on the base of the saucepan. Add Tabasco to taste, cool a little, then transfer to a blender and whiz until smooth. Keep warm until ready to serve.

FOR THE POTATOES Cut the potatoes into 1.5 cm (⅝ inch) wedges. Place in a saucepan of cold salted and bring to a simmer. Cook for 6–7 minutes, then strain and leave to cool.

Two-thirds fill a deep-fryer or large heavy-based saucepan with vegetable oil. Heat to 180°C (350°F), or until a cube of bread dropped into the oil turns golden brown in 15 seconds.

Dry the potato wedges with paper towel, then deep-fry for about 5–7 minutes, until golden and crisp. Season well with salt and pepper.

TO SERVE Spoon the tomato sauce onto a serving plate. Place the potato wedges on top, drizzle with the garlic aioli, garnish with the parsley and serve.

4 medium-sized waxy (boiling) potatoes, such as desiree or sebago
Garlic aioli (page 228), to serve
½ bunch flat-leaf (Italian) parsley, leaves only, roughly chopped

SPICY TOMATO SAUCE
1 onion, chopped
3 garlic cloves, chopped
1 tablespoon extra virgin olive oil
1 teaspoon sweet paprika
1 teaspoon smoked paprika
1 teaspoon ground cumin
pinch of chilli powder
200 g (7 oz) tinned whole tomatoes, chopped
2 teaspoons white sugar
2 teaspoons white wine vinegar
Tabasco or other hot sauce, to taste

All the elements of this dish look and taste fabulous together: the beetroot hummus adds such vibrant colour, and the sweetness of the honey is superb with haloumi. Serve this on its own as a light dish, or with duck cigars (page 186). Instead of haloumi, try saganaki cheese, cooked in the same way.

Honey & oregano haloumi with fig, golden beets, dandelion & walnuts

SERVES 4

8 baby golden beetroot (beets)
2½ tablespoons chardonnay vinegar
300 g (10½ oz) haloumi, cut into
    4 equal pieces
90 ml (3 fl oz/¼ cup) honey
1 teaspoon dried oregano
juice of 1 lemon
4 figs, halved
16 toasted walnuts
16 small dandelion leaves

BEETROOT HUMMUS
2 medium-sized beetroot (beets)
80 ml (2½ fl oz/⅓ cup) red wine
    vinegar
pinch of sea salt
100 g (3½ oz) tinned chickpeas,
    rinsed and drained
3 garlic cloves, roughly chopped
2 tablespoons tahini
1 tablespoon lemon juice
170 ml (5½ fl oz/⅔ cup) extra virgin
    olive oil

FOR THE BEETROOT HUMMUS Place the beetroot, vinegar and salt in a saucepan. Add enough water to cover the beetroot. Bring to the boil and cook for 20–30 minutes, until tender. Drain and cool slightly before peeling off the skin.

Place the beetroot in a food processor with the chickpeas, garlic, tahini and lemon juice and whiz to a smooth paste. With the motor running, slowly add the olive oil, processing until the mixture is thick and smooth. Season with salt and pepper.

FOR THE GOLDEN BEETS Place the golden beetroot and vinegar in a saucepan and cover with water. Cook for 10–15 minutes, or until the beetroot is soft. Strain and set aside to cool slightly, before rubbing off the skin with a clean cloth. Cut in half and set aside.

TO SERVE Heat a frying pan over medium–high heat. Add the haloumi and fry for 2 minutes on each side, or until well coloured. Add the honey, oregano and the golden beets and cook until the honey bubbles and has reduced a little. Add the lemon juice to deglaze the pan. Set aside.

Spoon the beetroot hummus onto a serving plate. Top with the haloumi and golden beets, then drizzle with the honey mixture from the pan. Arrange the figs alongside. Garnish with the toasted walnuts and dandelion leaves.

Packed full of flavour, these little chicken morsels make a terrific snack.
They are easy to prepare, and so much classier than regular fried chicken!

Crispy salt & pepper popcorn chicken

TO MARINATE THE CHICKEN Combine the marinade ingredients in a large bowl. Add the chicken pieces, making sure to completely coat them. Cover and marinate in the fridge for 30 minutes, or up to 1 hour.

TO FRY THE CHICKEN Two-thirds fill a deep-fryer or large heavy-based saucepan with vegetable oil. Heat to 170°C (325°F), or until a cube of bread dropped into the oil turns golden brown in 20 seconds.

Whisk the egg in a small bowl, and place the cornflour in a separate bowl.

Working in batches, dip the chicken pieces in the egg, then the cornflour, and place into the oil. Fry for 3–4 minutes, until golden. Remove with a slotted spoon and drain on paper towel.

Drop the fresh basil leaves into the oil for a few seconds, then remove.

TO SERVE THE CHICKEN Place the fried chicken in a serving dish. Sprinkle with the fried basil leaves and the five-spice powder. Toss to ensure all the chicken pieces are evenly coated.

Serve immediately, with the chipotle mayonnaise.

400 g (14 oz) boneless, skinless chicken thighs, cut into bite-sized pieces
vegetable oil, for deep-frying
1 free-range egg
125 g (4½ oz/1 cup) cornflour (cornstarch)
handful Thai basil leaves
1 tablespoon Chinese five-spice
Chipotle mayonnaise (page 226), to serve

SOY & SHAOXING MARINADE
2 garlic cloves, finely chopped
2 tablespoons soy sauce
1 tablespoon Chinese five-spice
½ teaspoon sesame oil
2 teaspoons shaoxing rice wine
½ teaspoon ground white pepper
⅛ teaspoon freshly ground black pepper
½ teaspoon sea salt
⅛ teaspoon white sugar

Chapter 4
Oysters & Sashimi

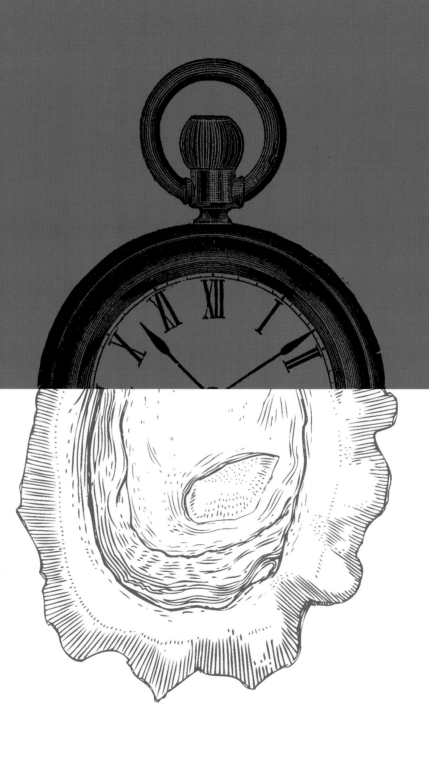

This would have to be one of my favourite chapters in the book, for the simple fact that most of the recipes require very little cooking, yet deliver a serious wow factor. I love their simplicity and how they let the produce be the star of the show.

The key thing is to get your hands on the freshest seafood you can. Make friends with your fishmonger and ask them about what's best to buy that day, and where their seafood comes from. And don't be afraid to ask them to slice, fillet and shuck your seafood for you.

Natural oysters with apple jelly (page 87) or fresh kingfish sashimi with nam jim, coconut yoghurt and toasted rice (page 95) make beautiful starters for a dinner party or gathering. For the slightly more adventurous, have a go at the herb-crumbed oysters with leek and tartare sauce (page 96), or the pizzettas with raw tuna, cavolo nero and spicy jalapeño (page 92).

The dishes in this chapter are made for sharing and are begging to be eaten outdoors on hot summer days, with a glass of wine in hand.

Our signature oyster dish, this one is on the menu at all our restaurants. You can buy wakame salad from sushi shops and some fish markets.

Tempura oysters with wakame salad, nori & wasabi

24 rock oysters, shucked
vegetable oil, for deep-frying
tapioca flour, for dusting
1 quantity Tempura batter (page 232)
rock salt, to serve
wakame salad, to serve
1 sheet nori, thinly sliced

WASABI DRESSING
1 tablespoon wasabi paste
250 ml (9 fl oz/1 cup) olive oil
3 teaspoons sesame oil
1 tablespoon soy sauce

FOR THE WASABI DRESSING Place the wasabi and 3 tablespoons hot water in a bowl and whisk until well combined.

Mix together the olive oil, sesame oil and soy sauce, then slowly add to the bowl in a steady stream, whisking until emulsified — be careful not to add the mixture too fast or the dressing will separate. Set aside.

FOR THE OYSTERS Remove the oysters from their shells and place the meat on a tray. Use paper towel to clean out the shells.

Two-thirds fill a deep-fryer or large heavy-based saucepan with vegetable oil. Heat to 170°C (325°F), or until a cube of bread dropped into the oil turns golden brown in 20 seconds.

Dust the oysters lightly in extra tapioca flour, then dip them into the tempura batter and lightly coat them. Working in two batches, deep-fry the oysters for about 1 minute, until golden. Drain on paper towel.

TO SERVE Make a bed of rock salt on a serving platter. Arrange the oyster shells on top. Spoon a little wakame salad into the shells, then drizzle with the wasabi dressing. Place an oyster on top of each and garnish with sliced nori.

If cutting your own kingfish, you'll need to use a really sharp knife to get very fine slices. You can also buy sashimi pre-cut from good fish markets.

Sashimi of kingfish with miso daikon, apple & coriander

SERVES 4

400 g (14 oz) sashimi-grade kingfish, blood line removed
1 green apple, cored and julienned
baby coriander (cilantro) leaves, to garnish

MISO DAIKON
50 g (1¾ oz) dashi powder
1 tablespoon light miso paste
1½ tablespoons dijon mustard
1½ tablespoons good-quality cabernet sauvignon vinegar
300 g (10½ oz) daikon, peeled and cut into 2.5 cm (1 inch) rounds

SOY & SESAME DRESSING
3 tablespoons organic soy sauce
4 teaspoons sesame oil
1½ tablespoons rice wine vinegar
3 teaspoons mirin
2 teaspoons plain Sugar syrup (page 232)
¼ piece dried kombu seaweed
3 tablespoons lime juice

FOR THE MISO DAIKON Combine the dashi powder and 250 ml (9 fl oz/1 cup) water in a saucepan and bring to a simmer. Slowly add the miso paste, mustard and vinegar, stirring to dissolve the miso. Add the daikon slices and simmer for 10–12 minutes, until tender.

Remove from the heat. Cover and refrigerate overnight.

The next day, strain the daikon, discarding the liquid. Cut into fine strips.

FOR THE SOY & SESAME DRESSING Combine the soy sauce, sesame oil, vinegar, mirin and sugar syrup in a saucepan. Place over medium heat until warm but not boiling. Remove from the heat, then stir in the seaweed and lime juice. Cover and set aside to cool.

TO SERVE Thinly slice the kingfish with a sharp filleting knife. Arrange the daikon strips in a line on a serving plate. Top with the kingfish slices. Drizzle the soy dressing over, garnish with the apple strips and coriander and serve.

I often reserve this recipe for treating guests, or for when I'm feeling a little adventurous. It is quite a fancy way of serving oysters, and makes a great shared starter or party canapé.

Natural oysters with apple jelly, pernod tapioca, salmon caviar & chives

MAKES 12

FOR THE APPLE JELLY Soak the gelatine sheets in cold water for 5 minutes.

Meanwhile, warm the apple juice in a saucepan to body temperature over medium heat. Remove from the heat.

Squeeze the excess water from the gelatine sheets, add them to the warm apple juice and stir until melted. Add the lemon juice. Strain to remove any gelatine that hasn't dissolved.

Pour into a small tray and refrigerate for 2–3 hours, until set.

FOR THE PERNOD TAPIOCA Bring a small saucepan of water to the boil, add the tapioca and cook for about 10–15 minutes, until the tapioca is completely transparent. Strain and rinse in cool water. Transfer to a bowl.

Stir in the Pernod and sugar syrup and refrigerate for 2 hours.

TO SERVE Make a bed of rock salt on a serving platter. Arrange the oysters on top. Use a fork to break up the apple jelly, then place about a teaspoon of the jelly onto each oyster. Top with the tapioca and salmon roe. Garnish with the chives and serve.

rock salt, for serving
12 oysters, shucked
2 tablespoons salmon roe
¼ bunch chives, finely chopped

APPLE JELLY
1⅓ sheets (4 g/⅛ oz) gelatine sheets (gold strength)
250 ml (9 fl oz/1 cup) clear apple juice
juice of ¼ lemon

PERNOD TAPIOCA
50 g (1¾ oz) tapioca pearls
1–1½ tablespoons Pernod
50 ml (1¾ fl oz) plain Sugar syrup (page 232)

If you like a really smoky flavour, leave the eggplant on the grill a little longer, for extra charring. The tzatziki and smoky eggplant also go wonderfully with barbecued lamb kebabs and warm pitta breads.

Oysters in chickpea batter with smoky eggplant & tzatziki

MAKES 12

12 oysters, shucked
plain (all-purpose) flour, for dusting
vegetable oil, for deep-frying
rock salt, for serving

TZATZIKI
125 g (4 oz/½ cup) plain yoghurt
¼ telegraph (long) cucumber
¼ garlic clove
1 teaspoon sea salt
½ teaspoon smoked paprika
¼ bunch dill, leaves only, chopped
handful mint leaves, chopped
juice of ½ lemon

SMOKY EGGPLANT
1 eggplant (aubergine), sliced in half
   lengthways
1 tablespoon lemon juice
2 tablespoons tahini
⅓ teaspoon ground cumin
⅓ teaspoon smoked paprika
2 tablespoons finely chopped flat-leaf
   (Italian) parsley

CHICKPEA BATTER
120 g (4¼ oz/1 cup) besan (chickpea flour)
250 g (9 oz/1⅔ cups) self-raising flour
2½ tablespoons cornflour (cornstarch)
¼ teaspoon ground cumin
pinch of bicarbonate of soda (baking soda)
pinch of sea salt
250 ml (9 fl oz/1 cup) lager

FOR THE TZATZIKI Line a colander with muslin (cheesecloth). Pour the yogurt into the cloth and tie together into a bundle, using kitchen string. Place in the fridge and leave to drain for 24 hours with a tray underneath to catch the draining liquid.

After draining for 24 hours, transfer the cheese to a bowl.

Remove the seeds from the cucumber and grate it, then place in a bowl with the yoghurt. Crush the garlic with the salt and add to the yoghurt, along with the remaining ingredients. Mix together, season with salt and pepper, then cover and refrigerate until required.

FOR THE SMOKY EGGPLANT Heat a chargrill pan or heavy-based frying pan over medium–high heat. Place the eggplant, skin side up, in the pan. Cook for 20 minutes, until soft and charred all over.

Set aside until cool enough to handle, then peel the skin off the eggplant and scoop out the flesh.

Place the eggplant flesh in a food processor. Add the remaining ingredients and process until smooth. Season with salt and pepper and set aside.

FOR THE CHICKPEA BATTER In a bowl, mix together the besan, flour, cornflour, cumin, bicarbonate of soda and salt. Slowly add the lager and mix to combine. Cover the bowl with a tea towel and rest in a warm place for 30 minutes before using.

FOR THE OYSTERS Remove the oysters from their shells and place the meat on a tray. Use paper towel to clean out the shells. Make a bed of rock salt on a serving platter and arrange the shells on top.

Two-thirds fill a deep-fryer or large heavy-based saucepan with vegetable oil. Heat to 180°C (350°F), or until a cube of bread dropped into the oil turns golden brown in 15 seconds.

Dust the oysters with flour, then dip them into the batter, ensuring they are well coated. Deep-fry the oysters for about 1 minute, until golden. Drain on paper towel.

TO SERVE Place a teaspoon of the smoky eggplant into each oyster shell. Top each shell with a warm oyster and a teaspoon of tzatziki and serve.

Spicy salmon with curry dressing, pear, frozen avocado & horseradish (page 93)

Oysters in chickpea batter with smoky eggplant & tzatziki (page 88)

Natural oysters with apple jelly, pernod tapioca, salmon caviar & chives (page 87)

Raw tuna pizzettas with cavolo nero, yellow tomatoes, jalapeño & wasabi (page 92)

Pizzetta is the Italian word for 'mini pizza'. I love this recipe because there are so many flavours and textures packed into one dish — the freshness of the tuna, mixed with spicy jalapeños, wasabi and the creaminess of the cavolo nero. These pizzettas are best served with an icy cold beer.

Raw tuna pizzettas with cavolo nero, yellow tomatoes, jalapeño & wasabi

MAKES 4 PIZZETTAS, YIELDING 16 SMALL PIECES

320 g (11¼ oz) sashimi-grade tuna loin

vegetable oil, for pan-frying

4 Peking duck pancakes, about 12 cm (4½ inches) round

2 small French shallots, sliced into thin rings

20 yellow cherry tomatoes, thinly sliced

1 jalapeño chilli, sliced into 10 thin rings

Wasabi dressing (page 233), for drizzling

extra virgin olive oil, for drizzling

4 tablespoons bonito flakes

baby coriander (cilantro) leaves, to garnish

CREAMED CAVOLO NERO

2 tablespoons unsalted butter

3 French shallots, finely chopped

1½ tablespoons plain (all-purpose) flour

250 ml (9 fl oz/1 cup) milk

½ teaspoon freshly ground nutmeg

400 g (14 oz) cavolo nero, ribs removed, leaves roughly chopped

FOR THE CREAMED CAVOLO NERO Melt the butter in a saucepan over medium heat. Add the shallot and cook for 3 minutes, until translucent. Add the flour and cook, stirring constantly, for 1 minute.

Add the milk and nutmeg. Season with salt and pepper. Increase the heat to high and cook, stirring, for 2 minutes, until the mixture has reduced by half.

Stir in the cavolo nero and cook for 3–4 minutes, until tender. Cool slightly, then place in a food processor and blend until smooth. Keep warm.

FOR THE TUNA Slice the tuna into four even pieces. Place each piece in between two pieces of plastic wrap and roll out to a 12 cm (4½ inch) round. Slice thinly using a sharp filleting knife.

TO SERVE Place a frying pan over low heat with a drizzle of vegetable oil. Add the pancakes and cook both sides until crispy. Drain on paper towel and transfer to a chopping board.

Spread each pancake with a thin layer of the creamed cavolo nero. Top with the shallot slices. Lay the tuna sashimi on top, then the tomato slices and jalapeño. Drizzle with some of the wasabi dressing, and a little extra virgin olive oil. Sprinkle with the bonito flakes and coriander.

Cut each pizzetta into four and serve.

Perfect with a glass of riesling, this is a really simple, light, flavoursome dish.
You can use ocean trout instead of the salmon if you wish.

Spicy salmon with curry dressing, pear, frozen avocado & horseradish

SERVES 4

Freeze the half avocado overnight.

Slice the salmon thinly, using a sharp filleting knife. Place on a serving plate and season with sea salt. Dress generously with the curry dressing and scatter the pear slices over the top.

Grate the frozen avocado and horseradish over the salmon, garnish with the Vietnamese mint and serve.

½ avocado
400 g (14 oz) sashimi-grade salmon, skin and blood line removed
Curry dressing (page 227), for drizzling
¼ nashi pear, thinly shaved
1 knob of fresh horseradish, peeled
handful Vietnamese mint leaves, torn

You can double the nam jim dressing quantity and keep the remainder in the fridge, where it will keep for up to a week. The dressing is also great drizzled over freshly shucked oysters, as well as Thai dishes.

Kingfish sashimi with nam jim, lime leaf, coconut yoghurt & toasted jasmine rice

SERVES 6

FOR THE TOASTED RICE Toast the rice in a dry frying pan over low heat for 2–3 minutes, until golden brown. Grind to a powder using a spice grinder or mortar and pestle. Store in an airtight container until required.

FOR THE NAM JIM DRESSING Roughly chop the chillies, garlic, ginger and coriander. Crush to a rough paste using a spice grinder or mortar and pestle, or chop as finely as possible.

Add the palm sugar in small amounts and mix until dissolved. Add the fish sauce and lime juice to taste.

TO SERVE Thinly slice the kingfish with a sharp filleting knife. Arrange the slices on a serving plate and season with sea salt. Drizzle with a generous amount of the nam jim dressing, then dot with the coconut yoghurt. Sprinkle with the lime leaf strips and toasted rice. Garnish with baby coriander to serve.

500 g (1 lb 2 oz) sashimi-grade
   kingfish, blood line removed
100 g (3½ oz) coconut yoghurt
3 kaffir lime leaves, thinly sliced
baby coriander (cilantro) leaves,
   to garnish

TOASTED JASMINE RICE
50 g (1¾ oz/¼ cup) jasmine rice

NAM JIM DRESSING
5 chillies (a mix of red and green)
1 garlic clove, peeled
1–2 cm (½ inch) piece of fresh ginger,
   peeled
5 coriander (cilantro) roots and
   stems, washed clean
100 g (3½ oz) palm sugar (jaggery),
   grated
3 tablespoons fish sauce
juice of 2–3 limes

If you have difficulty finding brioche crumbs, use panko crumbs — the large, flaky Japanese breadcrumbs sold in most supermarkets these days. The herb crumbs are also beautiful for coating chicken or veal schnitzels, while the herb paste is also wonderful with steak and fish.

Herb-crumbed oysters with leek & tartare sauce

MAKES 12

1 leek, white part only
12 medium-large oysters, shucked
plain (all-purpose) flour, for dusting
vegetable oil, for deep-frying
rock salt, for serving

HERB CRUMBS
100 g (3½ oz) brioche crumbs
¼ bunch flat-leaf (Italian) parsley, leaves only, chopped
¼ bunch tarragon, leaves only, chopped
¼ bunch mint, leaves only, chopped

HERB PASTE
1 tablespoon dijon mustard
1 teaspoon diced preserved lemon rind
1 teaspoon horseradish cream
2 free-range eggs

TARTARE SAUCE
25 g (1 oz) cornichons, finely chopped
¼ bunch flat-leaf (Italian) parsley, leaves only, chopped
¼ bunch tarragon, leaves only, chopped
¼ bunch dill, leaves only, chopped
2 hard-boiled free-range eggs, peeled and chopped
20 g (¾ oz) capers, finely chopped
20 g (¾ oz) Garlic confit (page 229), finely chopped
½ French shallot, finely chopped
1 tablespoon lemon juice
200 g (7 oz) mayonnaise

FOR THE LEEK Cut leek into quarters lengthways and slice thinly. Bring a small saucepan of salted water to the boil, add the leek and cook for 1 minute. Drain, then refresh in iced water. Drain again and dry with paper towel.

Place in a bowl and season with salt and pepper. Set aside.

FOR THE HERB CRUMBS Put all the ingredients in a blender and blitz until combined. Transfer to a tray and set aside.

FOR THE HERB PASTE Combine all the ingredients in a bowl and set aside.

FOR THE TARTARE SAUCE Combine all the ingredients in a bowl and set aside.

FOR THE OYSTERS Remove the oysters from their shells and place the meat on a tray. Use paper towel to clean out the oyster shells.

Dust the oysters with flour. Dip them into the herb paste, then into the herb crumbs, ensuring they are well coated.

Two-thirds fill a deep-fryer or large heavy-based saucepan with vegetable oil. Heat to 180°C (350°F), or until a cube of bread dropped into the oil turns golden brown in 15 seconds.

Deep-fry the oysters for about 1 minute, until golden. Drain on paper towel.

TO SERVE Make a bed of rock salt on a serving platter. Arrange the oyster shells on top. Spoon the leek into the shells, then top each shell with a crumbed oyster.

Serve with the tartare sauce on the side.

Chapter 5
Fish & Shellfish

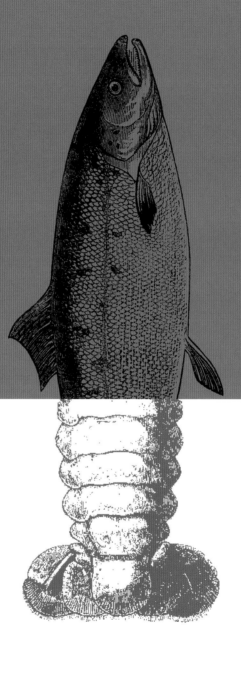

I've always loved cooking and preparing seafood; mind you, I've done my fair share of it. When I first started out at The Waterside Inn in Berkshire, England, I was assigned to fish butchery — long hours gutting, skinning and filleting fish, pretty much day in, day out, for six months. But these were the tools I needed to understand and respect the produce I was given.

In keeping with the theme of this book, I wanted to keep this chapter quite fun and relaxed, with most of the recipes designed for small bites and sharing.

For this chapter in particular, we've included dishes that are currently on our Salt tapas menus, some of which are so popular we just can't take them off; the prawn tempura tortillas with pineapple salsa (page 116) and salt cod croquettes with piccalilli (page 108) have always had our customers asking for more.

We've also put a bit of an Asian twist on a few classics — prawn toasts with smoked corn salsa and chipotle (page 105) and lobster milk buns with Vietnamese slaw (page 112) — and included some travel-inspired dishes, such as our grilled sardines with green tomato chutney and radish salad (page 126) and marinated anchovies with pico de gallo (page 110).

I hope you enjoy sharing these dishes as much as we do.

If you can't get hold of snow crab, try blue swimmer crab, which is available in larger supermarkets these days. These toasts make great bar snacks or canapés for a dinner party.

Devilled snow crab on toast

MAKES 10 PIECES

10 slices sourdough bread, cut into
    5 x 7 cm (2 x 2¾ inch) pieces
2½ tablespoons panko breadcrumbs
Chipotle mayonnaise (page 226),
    to serve
baby coriander (cilantro), to garnish

DEVILLED CRAB
250 g (9 oz) snow crab meat
2½ tablespoons mayonnaise
1 tablespoon diced French shallot
1 tablespoon finely chopped flat-leaf
    (Italian) parsley
1 tablespoon wasabi
2 teaspoons worcestershire sauce
dash of Tabasco sauce
pinch of cayenne pepper
1 tablespoon lemon juice

Preheat the oven to 180°C (350°F). Line a baking tray with baking paper.

Combine all the devilled crab ingredients in a bowl.

Toast the sourdough bread slices, and lightly toast the breadcrumbs in a dry frying pan.

Spread the sourdough toasts with the devilled crab mixture. Sprinkle with the breadcrumbs, then place on the lined baking tray. Bake for 3–4 minutes, to warm the crab mixture through.

Serve warm, with a little chipotle mayonnaise, topped with baby coriander.

For a perfect light brunch, snack or party canapé, use the English muffins recipe from page 54, but make them a little smaller for these elegant morsels. The spiced cucumber is also lovely with grilled or poached chicken or fish.

English muffins with swordfish, spiced cucumber & watercress

MAKES 8

FOR THE SPICED CUCUMBER Using a sharp knife, cut the cucumbers in half lengthways and scrape out the seeds. Cut on an angle into slices 4 mm (³⁄₁₆ inch) thick. Place in a bowl and add the onion, capsicum and salt. Mix well, then cover and refrigerate for 3 hours. Rinse and strain.

Combine the vinegar and turmeric in a saucepan and bring to the boil over medium–high heat. Add the sugar, cloves, mustard seeds and celery seeds and bring back to the boil. Remove from the heat and set aside to cool.

Pour the cooled pickling liquid over the cucumber mixture. Cover and marinate for at least 2 days in the fridge.

TO SERVE Heat a chargrill pan to high. Season the swordfish with salt and pepper and sear on each side for 3 seconds. Remove from the pan and sprinkle with the lime zest.

Cut the muffins in half and toast them in a toaster or under a grill (broiler) until golden brown. Spread a little crème fraîche over the bottom half of each muffin, then top with some watercress, the pickled cucumber, swordfish, and remaining crème fraîche.

Top with the muffin lids and serve warm.

320 g (11¼ oz) skinless swordfish loin, cut into 8 pieces
zest of 1 lime
8 mini English muffins (page 54)
2 tablespoons crème fraîche
watercress, to serve

SPICED CUCUMBER
2 small Lebanese (short) cucumbers (about 225 g/8 oz in total), peeled
¼ onion, sliced
¼ green capsicum (pepper), diced
2 teaspoons sea salt
115 ml (3¾ fl oz) white wine vinegar
¼ teaspoon ground turmeric
90 g (3¼ oz) brown sugar
¹⁄₁₆ teaspoon ground cloves
1½ teaspoons yellow mustard seeds
pinch of celery seeds

Rouille is a classic French garlic mayonnaise and is the perfect accompaniment to the crusted whiting fillets in this lovely tapas dish. Blood orange, when not in season, can be substituted with a good eating orange, such as navel or seville.

Turmeric & semolina-crusted whiting with fennel & blood orange salad

SERVES 4

2 free-range eggs
2½ tablespoons milk
8 small sand whiting fillets, scaled
100 ml (3½ fl oz) extra virgin olive oil
150 g (5½ oz) ghee or clarified butter

SAFFRON ROUILLE
pinch of saffron threads
100 ml (3½ fl oz) white wine
50 g (1¾ oz) warm cooked potato
1 free-range egg yolk
2 teaspoons dijon mustard
3 teaspoons lemon juice
40 g (1½ oz) Garlic confit (page 229)
200 ml (7 fl oz) extra virgin olive oil

TURMERIC & SEMOLINA SPICE MIX
1 tablespoon grated fresh turmeric
75 g (2½ oz) semolina
75 g (2½ oz) polenta
1½ teaspoons chilli powder
½ teaspoon cracked black pepper
1 tablespoon fine sea salt

FENNEL & BLOOD ORANGE SALAD
½ baby fennel, shaved, fronds
   reserved and finely chopped
1 blood orange, segmented,
   reserving any juices
¼ bunch dill, leaves only, torn
¼ bunch flat-leaf (Italian) parsley,
   leaves only, torn
1½ tablespoons extra virgin olive oil

FOR THE SAFFRON ROUILLE Combine the saffron and wine in a saucepan over medium heat. Leave to simmer away and reduce until you have only 1 tablespoon remaining. Pour into a bowl to cool.

Place the warm potato in a small food processor with the egg yolk, mustard, lemon juice and garlic confit. Process until smooth, slowly adding the olive oil and saffron-wine reduction in a steady stream. Season with salt and pepper.

FOR THE SPICE MIX Combine all the ingredients in a wide shallow bowl.

FOR THE SALAD Place all the ingredients in a bowl and toss to combine.

TO CRUST THE WHITING FILLETS Crack the eggs into a bowl, add the milk and whisk together. Check the whiting fillets have no small bones in them, then dip them in the egg mixture, then into the spice mixture, coating well. Place on a tray.

Heat the olive oil and ghee in a frying pan over medium heat. Add the fish and cook for 2 minutes on each side, until the fish is just cooked and light golden brown. Drain on paper towel.

TO SERVE Spoon the saffron rouille onto a serving plate, then arrange the fish fillets around. Top with the fennel and orange salad and serve.

These toasts are a great little snack or shared starter. It's really hard to stop at just one, so you might want to make extra...

Prawn toasts with smoked corn salsa & chipotle

MAKES 8 PIECES

FOR THE CORN SALSA Near serving time, cook the corn cob in a saucepan of salted boiling water for 5 minutes. Drain and refresh in ice-cold water, then pat dry. Cut the kernels off the husk and place in a bowl. Add the remaining ingredients and mix well. Season with salt and pepper.

FOR THE PRAWN MIX Place the prawn meat in a blender and whiz to a smooth paste. Add the remaining ingredients and blend to combine. Refrigerate until needed.

TO SERVE Two-thirds fill a deep-fryer or large heavy-based saucepan with vegetable oil. Heat to 180°C (350°F), or until a cube of bread dropped into the oil turns golden brown in 15 seconds.

Spread the bread slices with the prawn mix and sprinkle with the sesame seeds. Cut the crusts off the bread, then cut each piece in half.

Deep-fry the bread in batches for 2–3 minutes, or until golden all over. Drain on paper towel.

Place the warm toasts on a serving plate and top with the corn salsa. Drizzle with chipotle mayonnaise, garnish with the coriander and serve.

vegetable oil, for deep-frying
4 slices white bread
50 g (1¾ oz/⅓ cup) sesame seeds
Chipotle mayonnaise (page 226), to serve
handful coriander (cilantro) leaves, thinly sliced

CORN SALSA
1 corn cob
50 g (1¾ oz) French shallots, diced
1 teaspoon smoked paprika
handful coriander (cilantro) leaves, chopped
juice of ½ lime
3 tablespoons extra virgin olive oil

PRAWN MIX
250 g (9 oz) raw prawn meat
2 cm (¾ inch) piece of fresh ginger, peeled and chopped
1 garlic clove, chopped
½ teaspoon caster (superfine) sugar
½ teaspoon sea salt
1 free-range egg white
1 teaspoon sesame oil
2 tablespoons finely chopped spring onions (scallions)
1 teaspoon fish sauce

Salt cod croquettes with piccalilli
(page 108)

Prawn toasts with
smoked corn
salsa & chipotle
(page 105)

Marinated anchovies with pico de gallo (page 110)

Turmeric & semolina-crusted whiting with fennel & blood orange salad (page 104)

There is a bit of time involved in this dish, but the results are well worth it.
You can make the piccalilli up to a month in advance and keep it in an airtight
container in the fridge. It is great on roast beef sandwiches.

Salt cod croquettes with piccalilli

MAKES 12

vegetable oil, for deep frying
¼ bunch flat-leaf (Italian) parsley,
  leaves picked

PICCALILLI
200 g (7 oz) green (unripe) tomatoes,
  peeled, cored, and diced
¼ small cauliflower, cut into florets
½ Lebanese (short) cucumber, peeled
  and diced
½ green capsicum (pepper), diced
¼ onion, chopped
2 teaspoons sea salt
2 tablespoons brown sugar
1 teaspoon yellow mustard seeds
1 teaspoon celery seeds
½ teaspoon ground turmeric
2 teaspoons grated fresh horseradish
125 ml (4 fl oz/½ cup) white wine vinegar

SALT COD
250 g (9 oz) skinless, boneless salt cod
250 ml (9 fl oz/1 cup) milk
4 thyme sprigs
2 bay leaves
3 garlic cloves, lightly crushed

CROQUETTES
500 g (1 lb 2 oz) kipfler (fingerling) potatoes,
  peeled and cut into 5 cm (2 inch) pieces
2 tablespoons extra virgin olive oil
75 g (2½ oz) shallots, finely chopped
2 garlic cloves, finely chopped
¼ bunch coriander (cilantro), leaves only,
  chopped
½ teaspoon chopped, seeded red chilli
1 large free-range egg yolk, lightly beaten

CRUMBING MIXTURE
75 g (2½ oz/½ cup) plain (all-purpose) flour
1 free-range egg
3 tablespoons milk
200 g (7 oz) panko breadcrumbs

FOR THE PICCALILLI In a bowl, combine the tomatoes, cauliflower, cucumber, capsicum and onion. Toss the salt through and set aside for 3–4 hours. Drain thoroughly, then squeeze the vegetables to remove any excess liquid.

Place the sugar, spices, horseradish and vinegar in a saucepan over medium–high heat and simmer for 15 minutes. Add the drained vegetables and bring to the boil. Remove from the heat and cool.

When completely cool, transfer the piccalilli to a clean airtight container and refrigerate until required.

TO PREPARE THE SALT COD Put the fish in a bowl and cover with cold water. Leave to soak in the refrigerator for 24 hours, or for up to 2 days, changing the water at least three times during this time.

Drain the cod and transfer to a large saucepan. Add the milk, thyme, bay leaves and garlic. Pour in enough water to cover the fish by 5 cm (2 inches). Simmer over low heat for 20 minutes, or until the fish flakes when tested with a fork. Using a slotted spoon, transfer the cod to a plate and leave to cool, before breaking into flakes.

FOR THE CROQUETTES Cook the potatoes in a saucepan of boiling water until tender. Drain, transfer to a bowl and mash to a coarse purée.

Heat the olive oil in a saucepan over medium heat. Add the shallot and garlic and cook for 4 minutes, until the shallot has softened. Add to the bowl with the potatoes.

Add the cod flakes, coriander, chilli and egg yolk and stir until combined. Refrigerate for at least 30 minutes, until chilled.

Line a baking tray with baking paper. Shape about 1 tablespoon of the mixture into a log and place on the tray. Repeat with the remaining mixture, to make 12 logs.

FOR THE BREADCRUMB MIX Place the flour in a bowl. Lightly beat the eggs and milk in another bowl, and tip the panko crumbs into a third bowl.

Dip the croquette logs in the flour, then in the egg mixture, then coat with the panko crumbs. Arrange on a baking tray and refrigerate for 10 minutes until chilled.

TO SERVE Two-thirds fill a deep-fryer or large heavy-based saucepan with vegetable oil. Heat to 180°C (350°F), or until a cube of bread dropped into the oil turns golden brown in 15 seconds.

Working in batches, carefully lower the crumbed croquettes into the oil and cook for 3 minutes, until golden brown. Remove with a slotted spoon, drain on paper towel and leave to rest for 3 minutes.

Serve warm, garnished with parsley, with the piccalilli on the side.

Pico de gallo is a Mexican salsa, or fresh salad, that pairs wonderfully with these anchovies. Try it also with grilled chicken or steak, or just some fresh tortilla chips.

Marinated anchovies on sourdough with pico de gallo

MAKES 6

300 g (10½ oz) fresh anchovy fillets
125 ml (4 fl oz/½ cup) white wine
    vinegar
3 teaspoons sea salt
3 teaspoons dried oregano
3 teaspoons chilli flakes
2 garlic cloves, sliced paper-thin
⅓ bunch flat-leaf (Italian) parsley,
    leaves only, finely chopped
150 ml (5 fl oz) extra virgin olive oil
½ sourdough baguette, cut into
    6 slices

PICO DE GALLO
2 roma (plum) tomatoes
2 French shallots
1 jalapeño chilli
¼ bunch coriander (cilantro), leaves
    only, chopped
¼ bunch mint, leaves only, chopped
juice of 1 lime
½ teaspoon ground cumin
70 ml (2¼ fl oz) extra virgin olive oil
Tabasco or other hot sauce, to taste

FOR THE ANCHOVIES Place the anchovy fillets in a shallow dish and pour the vinegar over them. Cover and marinate in the refrigerator for at least 4 hours.

Drain the anchovies, rinse them, then pat dry with paper towel. Arrange on a tray in a single layer and sprinkle with the salt. Leave for 10 minutes.

In a bowl, combine the oregano, chilli flakes, garlic, parsley and olive oil. Pour the mixture over the anchovies. Cover and marinate in the fridge for 2–3 hours; the anchovies will keep for up to 1 week in the fridge.

FOR THE PICO DE GALLO Near serving time, chop the tomatoes, shallots and jalapeño into very small dice, leaving the seeds in your chilli if you like more spice. Place in a bowl, add the remaining ingredients and stir to combine. Season with salt and pepper to taste.

TO SERVE Remove the anchovies from the fridge, to bring them to room temperature; this will take about 30 minutes.

Toast the sourdough slices until golden brown.

Top the sourdough toasts with the pico de gallo, the anchovies, and a drizzle of the anchovy marinade. Serve immediately.

If fresh whitebait is not available, you can use frozen whitebait (from good fishmongers) for these dainty fritters.

Whitebait fritters with beetroot relish & dill crème fraîche

FOR THE FRITTERS Crack the eggs into a bowl and lightly beat. Add the flour and baking powder and mix to form a smooth batter. Fold in the whole whitebait fillets, herbs and lemon zest. Cover and refrigerate for 30 minutes.

FOR THE BEETROOT RELISH Place the honey and butter in a saucepan and cook over medium heat for 3–4 minutes, until a light caramel colour. Add the spices, cook for 30 seconds, then add the beetroot and cook for 4–5 minutes, until just tender. Stir in the vinegar and remove from the heat. Season with salt and pepper.

FOR THE DILL CRÈME FRAÎCHE Combine all the ingredients in a bowl. Season to taste and refrigerate until needed.

TO SERVE Heat a frying pan over medium heat and add a drizzle of grapeseed oil. Using 1 tablespoon of the whitebait batter for each fritter, cook several fritters at a time for 1½–2 minutes on each side. Drain on paper towel and keep warm while cooking the remaining fritters.

Serve the fritters warm, topped with the beetroot relish, dill crème fraîche and a drizzle of olive oil.

WHITEBAIT FRITTERS
2 free-range eggs
100 g (3½ oz/⅔ cup) self-raising flour
½ teaspoon baking powder
240 g (8½ oz) whitebait fillets
¼ bunch chives, snipped
¼ bunch flat-leaf (Italian) parsley, leaves only, chopped
zest of ¼ lemon
grapeseed oil, for pan-frying
extra virgin olive oil, for drizzling

BEETROOT RELISH
1½ tablespoons honey
1½ tablespoons unsalted butter
1 teaspoon ground ginger
1 teaspoon ground cinnamon
1 teaspoon ground allspice
1 teaspoon ground nutmeg
250 g (9 oz) beetroot, peeled and grated
1½ tablespoons sherry vinegar

DILL CREME FRAICHE
150 g (5½ oz) crème fraîche
2 tablespoons finely chopped dill
zest of ¼ lemon

Milk buns, sold in Asian bread shops, have a beautifully soft texture and are best served fresh and warm. Double the recipe quantities if feeding a crowd.

Milk buns with lobster & Vietnamese slaw

MAKES 4 BUNS

400 g (14 oz) live lobster, or
    precooked lobster
handful of salt
extra virgin olive oil, for drizzling
4 mini milk buns
½ quantity Miso mayo (page 230)

VIETNAMESE SLAW
60 g (2¼ oz) sugar
60 ml (2 fl oz/¼ cup) white vinegar
½ large carrot, cut into thin sticks
⅛ medium-sized daikon radish,
    cut into thin sticks
45 g (1¾ oz/1 cup) shredded Chinese
    cabbage
small handful coriander (cilantro)
    leaves, roughly torn
small handful mint leaves, roughly
    torn
¼ Lebanese (short) cucumber,
    sliced very thinly
1 red chilli, finely chopped

FOR THE SLAW In a small saucepan, combine the sugar, vinegar and 125 ml (4 fl oz/½ cup) water. Bring to the boil, pour into a bowl and cool.

Add the carrot, daikon and cabbage to the liquid and mix well. Season to taste with salt and pepper.

Transfer to an airtight container and marinate in the fridge for at least 2 hours, or overnight.

Just before serving, strain off the liquid, then mix the remaining ingredients through.

FOR THE LOBSTER If using a live lobster, place it in the freezer for 30 minutes to put it to sleep.

Place the lobster on a chopping board. Using a very sharp, strong knife, cut through the head, keeping the rest of the body intact.

Place a large pot of water on the stove over high heat. Add the salt, to resemble sea water, and bring to the boil. Add the lobster to the pot, reduce the heat to medium and cook for 6–7 minutes. Remove the lobster with a slotted spoon and refresh in iced water.

Use kitchen scissors to remove the cooked lobster head from the tail. Lay the body on its back and, using a strong, very sharp knife, cut it in half from the top of the tail to the bottom. Remove the flesh from the shell and discard the intestinal tract.

Cut the flesh into four medallions and drizzle with extra virgin olive oil. Season with salt and freshly cracked black pepper.

TO SERVE Cut the buns in half widthways. Spread 2 teaspoons of the miso mayonnaise on the bottom half of each bun. Top with a lobster medallion and the slaw. Put the bun lids on top and serve.

This simple summer dish is such a crowd pleaser. The flavoured butter can also be used on steaks, grilled fish or even crusty bread, and can be frozen for up to six months; just remove it from the freezer a day before using.

Split prawns with a garlic, dashi, chilli & lime butter

MAKES 8

FOR THE BUTTER Place the butter in a mixing bowl and whip until soft and pale, using electric beaters. Add the remaining ingredients and 2 teaspoons water and mix well.

Form into a log and wrap in plastic wrap. Chill in the refrigerator for at least 1 hour to firm up.

TO SERVE Preheat the grill (broiler) to high. Keeping the heads, tails and shells on, use a sharp knife to cut the prawns lengthways along the top, cutting almost all the way through. Open the prawns up, discard the intestinal vein and rinse with water.

Unwrap the butter and slice into eight pieces. Place the prawns on a heatproof tray, flesh side up, spread a piece of butter over each prawn and place under the grill. Cook for about 3–4 minutes, until the prawns have changed colour and are just cooked.

Serve on a platter with the lime halves.

8 large whole raw tiger prawns
4 limes, halved

GARLIC, DASHI, CHILLI & LIME BUTTER
140 g (5 oz) unsalted butter, at room temperature
30 g (1 oz) Garlic confit (page 229)
3 teaspoons dashi powder
1½ teaspoons chilli flakes
3 teaspoons sea salt
1½ teaspoons lime juice
large handful flat-leaf (Italian) parsley, leaves only, chopped

You'll find a great balance of flavours here — the sweetness of the pineapple and the heat from the chilli marry so well with tempura prawns. When in season, you can replace the pineapple with fresh peaches, nectarines or plums. The salsa is also great on grilled chicken. This recipe can easily be doubled.

Tempura prawn tortillas with pineapple salsa & chipotle mayo

MAKES 4 SMALL TACOS

4 small soft tortillas, cut to 10 cm
   (4 inch) rounds
2 iceberg lettuce leaves, thinly sliced
3 tablespoons Chipotle mayonnaise
   (page 226)
small handful coriander (cilantro)
   leaves

PINEAPPLE SALSA
125 g (4½ oz) pineapple, finely diced
1–2 chillies, seeded and finely diced
2 teaspoons white wine vinegar
2 teaspoons extra virgin olive oil
8 mint leaves, roughly chopped
8 coriander (cilantro) leaves, roughly
   chopped

TEMPURA PRAWNS
4 prawns
vegetable oil, for deep-frying
1 quantity Tempura batter (page 232)

FOR THE PINEAPPLE SALSA Near serving time, combine all the ingredients in a bowl, mixing well.

FOR THE TEMPURA PRAWNS Peel and devein the prawns, removing the tails. Cut a few small incisions on each side of each prawn so they don't curl up during cooking.

Two-thirds fill a deep-fryer or large heavy-based saucepan with vegetable oil. Heat to 170°C (325°F), or until a cube of bread dropped into the oil turns golden brown in 20 seconds.

Dip the prawns into the tempura batter, coating them evenly. Carefully lower the prawns into the oil and cook for 3–4 minutes. Drain on paper towel and season with salt and pepper.

TO SERVE While the tempura prawns are cooking, warm the tortillas briefly under a medium-hot grill (broiler), or for 10 seconds in a microwave.

Place the tortillas on a serving platter and add the lettuce and pineapple salsa. Top each with a tempura prawn, then drizzle with the chipotle mayonnaise. Serve garnished with the coriander.

Originating from Spain, padrón peppers are fat, sweet, generally mild green chillies that appear in fresh produce markets in summer. When not in season, use tinned piquillo peppers. If you can't get fresh scallops, buy frozen Japanese or Canadian scallops from good fishmongers for this tasty tapas dish.

Seared scallops with padrón peppers, fresh cheese, romesco & chorizo jam

SERVES 4

olive oil, for pan-frying
12 large scallops
12 padrón peppers
160 ml (5¼ fl oz) Romesco sauce (page 231)
small handful yellow celery leaves (from a celery heart)
extra virgin olive oil, for drizzling

FRESH CHEESE WITH ROSEMARY
500 ml (17 fl oz/2 cups) milk
125 ml (4 fl oz/½ cup) buttermilk
2½ tablespoons thick (double) cream
½ teaspoon sea salt
¼ lemon, peeled
2 rosemary sprigs
1 bay leaf, crushed

CHORIZO JAM
extra virgin olive oil, for pan-frying
75 g (2½ oz) French shallots, finely diced
150 g (5½ oz) fresh chorizo sausage, peeled and finely chopped; to make your own, see page 152
65 g (2¼ oz) sugar
150 ml (5 fl oz) apple juice
25 ml (¾ fl oz) sherry vinegar (preferably Pedro Ximénez)

FOR THE CHEESE Place all the ingredients in a saucepan over medium heat, whisking to combine. Remove from the heat just before the mixture comes to the boil. Set aside for 10 minutes.

Using a slotted spoon, carefully remove the solids from the top of the milk mixture and place in a piece of muslin (cheesecloth); discard the rosemary and bay leaf, and tie the muslin corners to enclose. Place the wrapped curd in a sieve over a bowl and leave in the fridge to dry for a minimum of 30 minutes. Discard any liquid.

FOR THE CHORIZO JAM Heat a splash of olive oil in a saucepan over medium heat. Add the shallot and cook for 2–3 minutes, until soft but not coloured. Add the chorizo and cook for another 5 minutes.

Now add the sugar and cook for another 2–3 minutes, then stir in the apple juice. Leave to cook, stirring now and then, for 20–25 minutes, until reduced to a jam consistency. Stir in the vinegar, remove from the heat and keep warm.

TO SERVE Heat a large frying pan over high heat. When hot, add a drizzle of olive oil. Add the scallops and peppers and cook for 1 minute on each side. Remove the scallops and drain on paper towel.

Reduce the heat to low and cook the peppers for another 1–2 minutes, shaking the pan so they cook all over. Drain on paper towel and season to taste with salt and pepper.

Spoon the romesco sauce around a serving platter, then top with the scallops. Dollop with the chorizo jam and fresh cheese. Garnish with the celery leaves and finish with a drizzle of extra virgin olive oil.

*You can use fresh butterflied sardines instead of garfish;
either way, this dish makes a lovely light, fresh starter.*

Grilled garfish with kohlrabi & fennel salad

FOR THE DRESSING Place all the ingredients in a blender and blitz until smooth. Pass through a fine sieve and chill until needed, but use on the same day it is prepared.

FOR THE GARFISH Lay the fish out on a tray and drizzle with a little olive oil. Sprinkle on both sides with the parsley, chilli and coriander seeds. Marinate in the fridge for 2 hours.

FOR THE KOHLRABI SALAD Preheat the oven to 150°C (300°F). Place the pine nuts on a baking tray and lightly toast in the oven for 4–6 minutes, or until golden. Tip into a bowl to cool.

Just before serving, place all the salad ingredients into a bowl and toss to combine.

TO SERVE Preheat a barbecue or chargrill pan to high. Place the garfish, skin side down, on the grill and cook for 1½ minutes. Remove to a serving plate. Season with salt and pepper.

Scatter the kohlrabi salad over the fish and garnish with baby sorrel leaves. Drizzle with the sorrel and apple dressing and serve.

4 garfish, butterflied
extra virgin olive oil, for drizzling
2–3 tablespoons flat-leaf (Italian) parsley leaves, finely chopped
1 red chilli, finely chopped
½ teaspoon coriander seeds, toasted and crushed
baby sorrel leaves, to garnish

SORREL & APPLE DRESSING
100 g (3½ oz) Lebanese (short) cucumber
125 ml (4 fl oz/½ cup) clear apple juice
1½ bunches sorrel leaves

KOHLRABI & FENNEL SALAD
40 g (1½ oz/¼ cup) pine nuts
¼ kohlrabi, peeled and thinly shaved
½ baby fennel bulb, thinly shaved
1 green apple, cored and shaved
1 tablespoon lemon juice
1½ tablespoons white balsamic vinegar
2 tablespoons extra virgin olive oil, plus extra for drizzling

A 'po boy' is a traditional sandwich from Louisiana and is wickedly addictive. These ones make a great bar snack with a cold beer. You can make the red pepper jam well ahead, and use any leftover on steak sandwiches and burgers.

Tempura mussel po boys

MAKES 8 PO BOYS

vegetable oil, for deep-frying
1 quantity Tempura batter (Basics, page 232)
80 g (2¾ oz/⅓ cup) Garlic aioli
   (page 228)
handful baby watercress leaves

RED PEPPER JAM
6 red capsicums (peppers)
2 teaspoons sea salt
165 g (5¾ oz/¾ cup) caster (superfine) sugar
2–3 red chillies, finely chopped
150 ml (5 fl oz) red wine vinegar

MUSSELS
32 large mussels, scrubbed well,
   hairy beards removed
1 teaspoon black peppercorns,
   lightly crushed
1 red chilli, sliced
2 coriander (cilantro) roots, washed well
   and roughly chopped
8 thyme sprigs
150 ml (5 fl oz) white wine

FRIED BREAD
2½ teaspoons dried yeast
350 ml (12 fl oz) warm water
500 g (1 lb 2 oz/3⅓ cups) plain
   (all-purpose) flour
½ teaspoon sea salt

FOR THE RED PEPPER JAM Finely chop the capsicums, discarding the seeds and white membranes. Place in a bowl, toss with the salt and set aside for 3 hours.

Transfer the mixture to a saucepan and add the sugar, chillies and vinegar. Gently cook over low heat for 1½ hours, until it has a jam-like consistency.

Leave to cool. If storing, seal in sterilised jars and keep in the fridge.

FOR THE MUSSELS Combine all the ingredients in a large bowl. Heat a large saucepan over high heat. When hot, add the mussel mixture and cover with a lid.

Cook for 2–3 minutes, or until the mussels have all opened. Strain and either discard the liquid, or reserve it to use in a fish-based soup.

Place the mussels on a tray and leave to cool in the fridge, before removing the mussels from their shells.

FOR THE FRIED BREAD Mix the yeast with the warm water, stirring until dissolved. Combine the flour and salt in a large bowl, add the yeast mixture and mix until well combined.

Tip onto a floured bench and knead for a few minutes, into a smooth dough. Cover with a tea towel and set aside in a warm place for 20 minutes.

Knead again for 2 minutes, then roll out to a 2.5 cm (1 inch) thickness and cut into 5 cm (2 inch) squares; you want to end up with eight squares.

Heat a heavy-based frying pan over medium–low heat. Add enough vegetable oil to come one-third of the way up the pan.

Heat the oil for 5 minutes, then carefully slide in the dough pieces and cook in batches for about 3 minutes on each side, or until golden brown. Drain on paper towel. Keep warm.

TO SERVE Two-thirds fill a deep-fryer or large heavy-based saucepan with vegetable oil. Heat to 180°C (350°F), or until a cube of bread dropped into the oil turns golden brown in 15 seconds.

Working in batches, dip the mussels in the tempura batter and deep-fry for about 3 minutes, until golden. Drain on paper towel.

Using a sharp knife, cut the fried bread in half through the side, so you have a top and bottom.

Place the bottom halves on a serving platter and divide the pepper jam, tempura mussels and garlic aioli among them.

Top with the watercress, then the bread lids, and serve.

Tempura mussel po boys (page 122)

A great starter with a glass of chilled white wine, this dish takes no time at all to prepare. I love how the radish salad adds a lovely crunch and texture to the sardines.

Grilled sardines with green tomato chutney & radish salad

4 fresh sardines, butterflied
125 g (4 oz/½ cup) Green tomato chutney (page 229)
125 g (4½ oz/½ cup) Garlic aioli (page 228)
extra virgin olive oil, to serve

RADISH SALAD
4 radishes, cut into sticks
¼ bunch flat-leaf (Italian) parsley, leaves only, roughly torn
3 tablespoons roughly torn fennel fronds
4 spring onions (scallions), thinly sliced
juice of 1 lemon
1½ tablespoons extra virgin olive oil

FOR THE SALAD Near serving time, mix all the ingredients together in a bowl, season with salt and pepper and set aside.

FOR THE SARDINES Preheat a barbecue or chargrill pan to high.

Lay the sardines on a tray, drizzle with olive oil and season with salt and pepper.

When the barbecue or grill pan is hot, add the sardines, skin side down, and cook, without turning them over, for 45 seconds to 1 minute, until the sardines are half cooked. Remove from the grill; the residual heat will continue to cook them. Keep warm.

TO SERVE Lightly warm the chutney to just above room temperature. Spread the chutney on a serving plate and lay the sardines on top.

Dollop the garlic aioli around the sardines. Scatter the radish salad over. Drizzle with olive oil and serve.

Grilled chorizo and octopus are a match made in heaven. Serve as a tapas dish with crusty bread, to soak up all those flavoursome juices.

Grilled chorizo & octopus with piquillo peppers & apple & ginger purée

SERVES 4

FOR THE CRUSTY BREAD Preheat the oven to 150°C (300°F). Place the bread on a baking tray and drizzle with olive oil. Bake for 10–15 minutes, or until crisp and golden. Set aside to cool completely.

FOR THE APPLE & GINGER PUREE Place the apples, ginger, sugar and 300 ml (10½ fl oz) water in a saucepan over medium heat. Cook for 10–15 minutes, or until there is no liquid remaining.

Add the cream, reduce the heat, and warm through for 2 minutes.

While still warm, transfer to a blender and whiz until smooth. Push the mixture through a fine sieve and keep warm.

TO SERVE Preheat a barbecue or chargrill pan to medium. Drizzle with olive oil.

Cut each chorizo into five pieces and place on the barbecue with the piquillo peppers, whole chillies and baby octopus. Cook for 4–6 minutes, turning halfway through. Transfer to a tray and season with salt and pepper.

Spoon the warm apple and ginger purée onto a serving plate. Arrange the chorizo, octopus, piquillo, chillies and crusty bread on the plate. You are aiming for a rustic look!

Garnish with the fennel fronds and drizzle with a little more extra virgin olive oil. Serve warm.

4 thin slices crusty white bread, torn
extra virgin olive oil, for drizzling
2 chorizo sausages; to make your own, see page 152
6 pieces tinned piquillo peppers, cut in half
4 long red chillies
300 g (10½ oz) baby octopus, cleaned and cut in half
fennel fronds, to garnish

APPLE & GINGER PUREE
250 g (9 oz) apples, cored and diced
6 cm (2½ inch) piece of fresh ginger, peeled and grated
40 g (1½ oz) caster (superfine) sugar
2 tablespoons thick (double) cream

Chapter 6
Meat

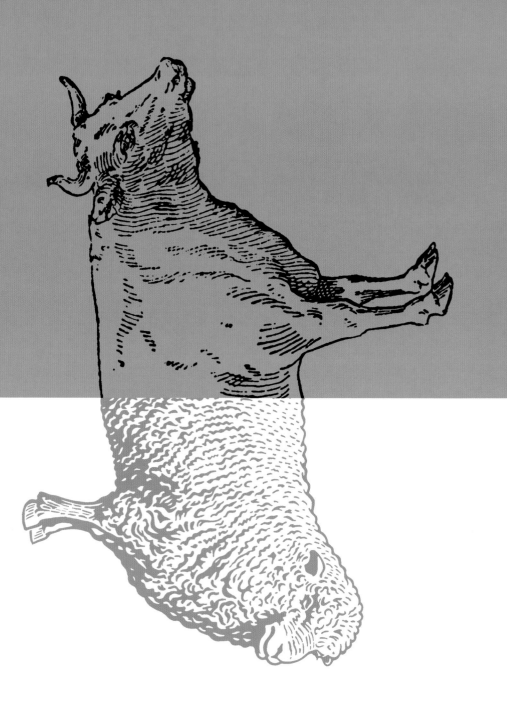

I've never really been one for food trends; I believe in good, honest food that's approachable for everyone. Sometimes the simplest of dishes are the ones you keep coming back to. I remember my first trip to New York, with a couple of my chefs. When we arrived we headed straight to Balthazar Restaurant, where we dined on a simple plate of steak and frites, with béarnaise sauce and beautiful red wine, and still to this day it's one of my most memorable meals — nothing fancy, just good food shared amongst friends.

This chapter includes a good mix of smaller and larger dishes. You'll find some great small bites and party fare in grass-fed beef sliders (page 166) and mini corned beef and crab sandwiches (page 133). For more main-meal dishes, try the fragrant chermoula lamb with pumpkin couscous (page 144), or a wickedly good plate of sticky glazed pork spare ribs (page 155).

Not many people know this about me, but I used to make and sell my own sausages before the days of owning my own restaurants. It was a great little business. We'd sell four different types of sausages at growers' markets, and they became pretty popular — at one stage we were selling about 1000 kilos of sausages a week! So I've also included recipes for my merguez sausages (page 162) and homemade chorizo (page 152) for you to share with friends and family.

Look for horseradish in the mustard and sauces section of delis and supermarkets. It adds a tasty bite to these simple toasted sandwiches.

Mini corned beef & crab sandwiches

FOR THE COCKTAIL SAUCE Combine all the ingredients and set aside. (If making the sauce ahead of time, it will keep covered in the fridge for up to 1 week; bring to room temperature for serving.)

FOR THE SANDWICHES Preheat the grill (broiler) to high.
    Combine the green and red cabbage in a bowl. Add half the cocktail sauce, season with salt and pepper, toss together and set aside.
    In a separate bowl, place the crabmeat and remaining cocktail sauce. Season, mix well to combine and set aside.
    Toast the bread slices under the grill until golden.

TO SERVE Place four slices of toast on serving plates. Top with the cabbage mixture, then the silverside and the crab mixture. Add the gherkin slices and sandwich the remaining toast slices on top. Serve immediately.

80 g (2¾ oz/1 cup) finely shredded green cabbage
80 g (2¾ oz/1 cup) finely shredded red cabbage
160 g (5½ oz) crabmeat
8 slices rye bread, each about 1 cm (½ inch) thick
150 g (5½ oz) good-quality silverside, thinly sliced
1 large gherkin (pickle), thinly sliced lengthways

COCKTAIL SAUCE
100 g (3½ oz) whole-egg mayonnaise
2½ tablespoons tomato sauce (ketchup)
2 tablespoons horseradish relish
25 g (1 oz) French shallot, finely diced
2 teaspoons Cognac
a few drops of Tabasco or other hot sauce
2 teaspoons worcestershire sauce
3 teaspoons lemon juice

I don't think there's anything more satisfying than a hot, freshly made empanada — travelling through Spain, I had one in my hands most days. A classic tapas dish, empanadas also make a great bar snack with a glass of Spanish white wine such as albariño. Instead of lamb, you can use beef, pork or even chicken in these empanadas.

Spiced lamb empanadas with tomato chutney & basil mayo

MAKES 10 EMPANADAS

4 sheets puff pastry
plain (all-purpose) flour, for dusting
1 free-range egg, lightly beaten
Green tomato chutney (page 229),
    to serve

LAMB FILLING
olive oil, for pan-frying
2 French shallots, finely diced
2 teaspoons ras el hanout (a North
    African spice blend, from spice
    shops and good food stores)
2 teaspoons oregano leaves
200 g (7 oz) minced (ground) lamb
1 free-range egg, lightly beaten
3 tablespoons pouring (single) cream

BASIL MAYONNAISE
200 g (7 oz) whole-egg mayonnaise
12 basil leaves, thinly sliced

FOR THE LAMB FILLING Heat a splash of olive oil in a frying pan over medium heat. Add the shallot and cook for 3–4 minutes. Add the ras el hanout and oregano and cook for another 30 seconds. Transfer to a bowl and leave to cool.

Add the lamb, egg and cream to the bowl. Mix through and season with salt and pepper.

FOR THE EMPANADAS Lay the pastry sheets on a floured bench. Cut 10 rounds out of each sheet, using a coffee mug or sturdy glass. Brush the pastry rounds with some of the beaten egg.

Spoon 1 tablespoon of the lamb filling onto each round and fold the pastry over to make a half-moon shape. Squeeze the pastry edges together with your fingers to seal them.

FOR THE BASIL MAYONNAISE Just before serving, combine the mayonnaise and basil in a bowl.

TO SERVE Preheat the oven to 180°C (350°F).

Place the empanadas on a baking tray and brush each with the remaining beaten egg. Bake for 20–25 minutes, or until golden brown.

Rest the empanadas for 5 minutes, then serve with tomato chutney and the basil mayonnaise.

This is a lovely light starter for a dinner party. You can easily increase the quantity if you are serving this for a group.

Spiced grass-fed beef tartare with almonds & sultanas

SERVES 4

2 tablespoons slivered almonds
2 teaspoons sultanas (golden raisins)
80 ml (2½ fl oz/⅓ cup) port
2 garlic cloves, finely diced
125 ml (4 fl oz/½ cup) extra virgin
   olive oil, plus extra for drizzling
1 teaspoon ground cinnamon
1 teaspoon ground allspice
1 teaspoon sumac
280 g (10 oz) very fresh grass-fed
   beef fillet
2 teaspoons Cognac
2 French shallots, finely diced
handful mint leaves, chopped
1 tablespoon lime juice
4 tablespoons coriander (cilantro)
   leaves, very roughly chopped
1 free-range egg yolk
8 grilled or toasted sourdough slices

Preheat the oven to 160°C (315°F).

Spread the slivered almonds on a small baking tray and bake for 6–8 minutes, or until golden. Tip into a bowl to cool.

Meanwhile, place the sultanas in a small bowl. Bring the port to a simmer in a saucepan over medium heat, then pour the warm port over the sultanas. Stir to combine and set aside to cool. Drain the sultanas, reserving the port for another use, and roughly chop them.

Place the garlic, olive oil, cinnamon, allspice and sumac in a saucepan over medium heat and cook for 30 seconds, until the spices start sizzling. Remove from the heat and set aside to cool.

Using a very sharp knife, chop the beef into very small pieces and place in a bowl. Pour the cooled spice mixture over. Add the Cognac, shallot, mint, lime juice and the chopped sultanas. Season with salt and pepper and stir to combine.

TO SERVE Spoon the beef mixture onto a serving plate. Garnish with the toasted almonds and chopped coriander. Top with the egg yolk, drizzle with a little more extra virgin olive oil and season with salt and pepper. Serve immediately, with the sourdough toasts.

Simple and stylish, here's a quick weeknight meal that pairs nicely with the Moroccan cauliflower salad on page 72. The raisin and caper purée is a good mix of salty and sweet, and also works well with spatchcock and quail.

Moroccan lamb cutlets with raisin & caper purée, broccolini & hazelnuts

SERVES 6

FOR THE RAISIN & CAPER PUREE Combine the raisins and capers in a saucepan with 75 ml (2¼ fl oz) water and bring to the boil. Reduce the heat and simmer for 5 minutes, then remove from the heat to cool slightly.

Blend until smooth, then push the mixture through a fine sieve. Set aside.

TO SERVE Heat a barbecue or chargrill pan to medium–high.

Drizzle the lamb and broccolini with olive oil and sprinkle with the spice mix, ensuring everything is well coated. Season with salt and pepper.

Grill the lamb for 2 minutes on each side, then set aside to rest. Meanwhile, grill the broccolini for 2–3 minutes on each side, until just cooked.

Spoon the raisin and caper purée onto a serving platter. Arrange the lamb and broccolini over the top. Garnish with the toasted hazelnuts and serve.

12 lamb cutlets, trimmed
2 bunches broccolini
extra virgin olive oil, for drizzling
3 tablespoons Moroccan spice mix
3 tablespoons hazelnuts, toasted and peeled

RAISIN & CAPER PUREE
150 g (5½ oz) raisins
35 g (1¼ oz) capers

Bacon-wrapped scallops with green tomato chutney & blackened lime (page 142)

Beef short ribs with Pedro Ximénez, roasted red onion and carrot & cumin purée (page 140)

Moroccan lamb cutlets with raisin & caper purée, broccolini & hazelnuts (page 137)

Spiced grass-fed beef tartare with almonds & sultanas (page 136)

A glass of shiraz or cabernet goes perfectly with this great slow-cooked winter dish. Why not roast some extra onions at the same time, to use in other dishes.

Beef short ribs with Pedro Ximénez, roasted red onion & carrot & cumin purée

SERVES 4

500 g (1lb 2 oz) beef short ribs
vegetable oil, for pan-frying
¼ carrot, sliced
¼ onion, sliced
7.5 cm (3 inch) piece of celery, sliced
2 garlic cloves, crushed
2 thyme sprigs
2 rosemary sprigs
¼ teaspoon cracked black pepper
100 g (3½ oz) tinned whole tomatoes
    (including juice)
200 ml (7 fl oz) red wine
300 ml (10½ fl oz) good-quality beef stock
80 ml (2½ fl oz/⅓ cup) Pedro Ximénez
    sherry vinegar
2 tablespoons chopped tarragon leaves
50 g (1¾ oz) piece of fresh horseradish,
    peeled
½ bunch chives, cut into batons

ROASTED RED ONION
1 red onion, skin on, cut in half
1 tablespoon extra virgin olive oil
1 tablespoon balsamic vinegar

CARROT & CUMIN PUREE
3 medium carrots, peeled and sliced
1 garlic clove, thinly sliced
1 teaspoon cumin seeds
2 teaspoons extra virgin olive oil
1 tablespoon unsalted butter
150 ml (5 fl oz) pouring (single) cream

FOR THE BEEF Preheat the oven to 130°C (250°F). Heat a heavy-based frying pan over high heat. Drizzle with a little vegetable oil.

Season the ribs with salt and pepper and add them to the frying pan. Cook for 6–8 minutes, turning to brown all over. Transfer to a small baking dish.

Using the same pan, drizzle in a little more oil and heat again over medium–high heat. Add the vegetables and garlic and cook, stirring now and then, for 5 minutes, until well coloured. Add the herbs, season with salt and the black pepper, and cook for another 2 minutes.

While the vegetables are browning, roughly blend the tomatoes with the juice in a food processor.

Add the wine to the pan and allow to reduce by half, then add the stock and the tomatoes. Bring to a simmer, remove from the heat and pour over the ribs.

Cover with foil and transfer to the oven. Bake for 2–2½ hours, or until the meat is tender.

Remove the ribs from the baking dish and keep warm. Strain the liquid through a fine sieve, then pour into a saucepan. Place over medium heat and allow to reduce by two-thirds, to a sauce consistency. Stir in the vinegar and tarragon, then add the ribs to the sauce.

FOR THE ROASTED ONION While the ribs are in the oven, place the onion, cut side down, on a small roasting tray. Drizzle with the olive oil and vinegar, and season with salt and pepper. Cover the tray with foil, then transfer to the oven.

Roast for about 45 minutes, or until the onion is tender and caramelised. Remove from the oven and allow to cool. Peel off the skin and cut the onion into quarters.

FOR THE CARROT & CUMIN PUREE Combine the carrot, garlic, cumin seeds, olive oil and butter in a saucepan over medium heat. Cook for 15 minutes, or until the carrot is tender. Add the cream, season, then cover and cook for another 5 minutes.

Transfer to a blender and whiz to a smooth purée. Place the purée in a clean saucepan, ready for reheating.

TO SERVE Gently reheat the carrot purée and place a few dollops onto a serving platter. Place the short ribs next to the purée and arrange the onion quarters around. Grate the fresh horseradish over top, garnish with the chives and serve.

Scallops and bacon taste exquisite together: you get the sea freshness from the scallop and the lovely flavour and fattiness of the bacon, brightened here with a slightly tart chutney. Using fresh seasonal scallops, rather than frozen, will make all the difference to this simple tapas dish.

Bacon-wrapped scallops with green tomato chutney & blackened lime

SERVES 4

12 fresh scallops, roe on or off
12 slices pancetta
extra virgin olive oil, for pan-frying
    and drizzling
2 limes, halved
½ quantity Green tomato chutney
    (page 229)
1 green apple, cored and julienned
¼ bunch chives, finely chopped

Place the scallops on a clean chopping board. Wrap one slice of pancetta around each scallop and place a toothpick through the pancetta and scallop to hold it together.

Heat a splash of olive oil in a frying pan over medium heat. Cook the scallops for 40 seconds on each side, taking care that the pancetta doesn't burn, or fall off during turning. Transfer the scallops to a tray.

Place the lime halves flat side down in the pan and cook until the surface turns black. Set aside.

TO SERVE Spoon the green tomato chutney into the centre of a serving platter, then arrange the scallops around the plate. Scatter with the apple and chives and drizzle with olive oil. Serve with the blackened lime halves for squeezing over.

Ideal for grilling, stewing or braising, ox tongue is a great-value meat. Ajvar (pronounced ay-var) is a Slavic red pepper relish that is also lovely with homemade sausages (pages 152 and 162) or as a dip with crusty bread.

Grilled beef ox tongue with ajvar & dill pickle

SERVES 4

FOR THE AJVAR Heat a chargrill pan or barbecue to medium–high. Season the capsicums and chillies with salt and pepper. Chargrill, turning regularly, for 20 minutes, or until black and blistered; the chillies will blacken more quickly than the capsicum. Transfer to a bowl and cover with plastic wrap to sweat.

Chargrill the eggplant for about 20 minutes, until blackened. Leave to cool, uncovered, in a clean bowl.

Skin and seed the capsicums; place the flesh in a blender with the chillies and garlic. Add the eggplant flesh. Turn the blender on and slowly add the lemon juice and olive oil in a steady steam. Transfer to a container, season to taste and set aside.

FOR THE OX TONGUE Heat a heavy-based saucepan over medium–high heat for a few minutes. Add the vegetable oil, carrot, onion and celery and cook, stirring, for 3 minutes. Stir in the herbs, peppercorns and the white and red wines. Cook, stirring occasionally, until the liquid has reduced down to one-third.

Add the stock and bring to a simmer. Add the tongue, cover and simmer gently for 1½ hours, or until tender; take care not to over-braise the meat. Take the pan off the heat to cool for about 10 minutes.

Remove the tongue from the liquid and place on a tray. While still warm, peel off the outer skin, then cut widthways into about thin 12 slices.

TO SERVE Heat a barbecue or chargrill to medium–high. Season the tongue slices, then sprinkle all over with the five-spice and olive oil. Chargrill on each side for 2 minutes. Spread the ajvar on a platter, top with the tongue slices, pickles and dill and serve as a tapas.

AJVAR
450 g (1 lb) red capsicums (peppers)
4 whole mild or hot red chillies
1 eggplant (aubergine)
1 garlic clove, crushed
juice of ½ lemon
60 ml (2 fl oz/¼ cup) olive oil

OX TONGUE
1 beef ox tongue, soaked in salted
    cold water for 24 hours
100 ml (3½ fl oz) vegetable oil
1 small carrot, roughly chopped
1 onion, roughly chopped
2 celery stalks, roughly chopped
5 bay leaves
½ bunch thyme
1 teaspoon black peppercorns
300 ml (10½ fl oz) white wine
300 ml (10½ fl oz) red wine
1 litre (35 fl oz/4 cups) veal stock

TO SERVE
2 teaspoons Chinese five-spice
extra virgin olive oil, for drizzling
2 dill pickles (gherkins), thinly sliced
½ bunch dill, leaves picked

Chermoula is a blend of spices and is the original seasoning for grilled meats and fish in Moroccan cuisine. It is magical with these lamb loins, which make a great sharing dish paired with a colourful couscous and a minted yoghurt spiked with harissa, a fiery Tunisian chilli paste.

Chermoula lamb loin with pumpkin couscous & harissa yoghurt

SERVES 6

30 g (1 oz) chermoula
6 x 80 g (2¾ oz) lamb loins, trimmed
1½ tablespoons extra virgin olive oil
coriander (cilantro) leaves, to garnish

PUMPKIN COUSCOUS
350 g (12 oz) butternut pumpkin,
  peeled, seeded and cut into 2 cm
  (¾ inch) cubes
extra virgin olive oil, for drizzling
100 g (3½ oz) podded fresh peas
  (or frozen would be fine)
95 g (3¼ oz/½ cup) couscous
125 ml (4 fl oz/½ cup) orange juice
1 tablespoon lemon thyme leaves
¼ bunch coriander (cilantro), leaves
  only, roughly chopped
3 tablespoons chardonnay vinegar

HARISSA YOGHURT
260 g (9¼ oz/1 cup) Greek-style
  yoghurt
2 heaped tablespoons harissa
1½ tablespoons lime juice
½ bunch mint, leaves only,
  finely chopped

FOR THE LAMB Rub the chermoula all over the lamb. Cover and refrigerate until ready to serve.

FOR THE COUSCOUS Preheat the oven to 180°C (350°F).
    Place the pumpkin on a baking tray, drizzle with olive oil and season with salt and pepper. Bake for 30 minutes, or until soft and golden.
    Meanwhile, half-fill a small saucepan with water and bring to the boil. Add the peas and cook for 30 seconds, then remove with a slotted spoon and place into a bowl of iced water. Once cooled, strain and set aside.
    Place the couscous in a bowl. In a saucepan, bring the orange juice to the boil, add the lemon thyme leaves and pour over the couscous. Cover and set aside for 10 minutes.
    Use a fork to fluff up and separate the couscous grains. Add the peas, roasted pumpkin, coriander and vinegar. Drizzle with more olive oil, season and mix well.

FOR THE HARISSA YOGHURT Mix all the ingredients together and set aside.

TO SERVE Heat the olive oil in a frying pan over medium heat. Cook the lamb for 3–4 minutes on each side for medium, or until cooked to your liking. Remove from the heat and leave to rest for 3 minutes, then thickly slice each lamb loin.
    Place the couscous on a platter or serving plates and top with the lamb. Add a dollop of the harissa yoghurt and serve garnished with coriander leaves.

These savoury morsels make a handsome canapé for a party.
Cut them into smaller bite-sized pieces if you prefer.

Lamb in puff pastry with mushroom duxelles & dried black olives

MAKES 16 PIECES

TO DRY THE OLIVES Preheat the oven to 60°C (140°F). Line a tray with baking paper.

Pit the olives and place on the lined baking tray. Bake for 4 hours, until all the moisture has been drawn out of them. Remove from the oven and set aside.

FOR THE MUSHROOM DUXELLES Heat the olive oil in a frying pan over medium–high heat. Add the mushrooms and cook, stirring, for 5–8 minutes, or until all the liquid has evaporated.

Add the thyme and wine and cook until there is no liquid remaining.

Leave to cool, then blend in a food processor until you have a coarse paste. Season with salt and pepper, fold the chopped black olives through and set aside.

FOR THE LAMB PARCELS Cut the puff pastry sheets slightly larger than the lamb fillets, keeping enough width to completely enclose the lamb and filling.

Spread the mushroom mixture on one side of each piece of lamb. Place the lamb on the cut pastry. Brush the pastry edges with the beaten egg, then roll up like a sausage roll. Press the pastry edges together to seal.

Pour olive oil to a depth of 5 mm (¼ inch) into a frying pan to shallow-fry the lamb parcels. Place over medium heat. When the oil is hot, add the lamb parcels and cook until dark golden on all sides. This will take 1½ minutes on each of the four sides. Remove from the heat and leave to rest for 2 minutes.

TO SERVE Cut each lamb parcel into four slices and serve warm, garnished with the dried olives.

160 g (5½ oz/1 cup) kalamata olives
4 sheets puff pastry
4 x 80 g (2¾ oz) lamb fillets or tenderloins, trimmed
1 free-range egg, beaten
extra virgin olive oil, for shallow-frying

MUSHROOM DUXELLES
2½ tablespoons extra virgin olive oil
300 g (10½ oz) button mushrooms, sliced
4 thyme sprigs, leaves picked
400 ml (14 fl oz) red wine
80 g (2¾ oz/½ cup) pitted black olives, chopped

If time permits, make the beef koftas a day in advance to allow the flavours to develop and the meat to firm up in the fridge. This is a fun dish to serve in the middle of the table, letting everyone fill their own lettuce cups.

Thai beef koftas in lettuce cups with coconut sauce

MAKES 4 LETTUCE CUPS

extra virgin olive oil, for drizzling
4 iceberg lettuce leaf cups
½ bunch coriander (cilantro), leaves only
1 lime, cut into quarters

THAI BEEF KOFTAS
1 garlic clove, crushed
1 teaspoon grated fresh ginger
2 teaspoons lime juice
2 teaspoons fish sauce
2 teaspoons soft brown sugar
2 teaspoons Thai red curry paste
chopped red chilli, to taste
320 g (11¼ oz) minced (ground) beef

COCONUT SAUCE
125 ml (4 fl oz/½ cup) coconut yoghurt
2 teaspoons Thai red curry paste
2 teaspoons lime juice
2 teaspoons fish sauce
3 teaspoons soft brown sugar
1 teaspoon soy sauce
1 teaspoon sesame oil
1 tablespoon finely chopped coriander (cilantro)

FOR THE KOFTAS Soak four wooden skewers in cold water for 1 hour.

Meanwhile, preheat a chargrill pan or barbecue to medium–high.

In a bowl, combine the garlic, ginger, lime juice, fish sauce, sugar and curry paste, adding chilli to taste. Add the beef and mix with your hands until well combined.

Divide the mixture into four equal portions, then roll each portion into a long sausage shape. Push a wooden skewer through the centre of each and drizzle with olive oil.

Grill for 8–10 minutes, turning the skewers every 2 minutes or so, until the koftas are completely cooked through.

FOR THE COCONUT SAUCE Combine all the ingredients in a bowl.

TO SERVE Remove the koftas from the skewers and place on a serving platter, along with the coconut sauce, lettuce cups, coriander and lime wedges.

To eat, place a kofta in a lettuce cup and drizzle with the coconut sauce. Squeeze some lime juice over the top, then roll up and devour.

Hailing from Italy, bresaola is beef that has been flavoured with wine and spices, then hung up to cure and air-dry for up to three months. Here it elevates a very simple tapas dish to almost superstar status. You'll find stracciatella, a soft, fresh shredded Italian buffalo-milk cheese, in good delicatessens or fine food stores, or try fresh burrata cheese instead. If plums are not in season, a nashi pear would work well.

Wagyu bresaola bruschetta with stracciatella, blood plum & fennel cress

MAKES 6

Toast the sourdough slices and arrange on a large serving platter.

Top with the stracciatella, sprinkle with the shichimi and season with salt and pepper.

Arrange the plum slices on top and garnish with the fennel cress. Place the bresaola next to the toasts and serve.

6 slices sourdough bread
200 g (7 oz) stracciatella cheese, strained well through a fine sieve
½ teaspoon shichimi togarashi (Japanese seven-spice, from Asian supermarkets)
2 blood plums, flesh thinly sliced
1 punnet fennel cress or fennel fronds
12 long, thin slices wagyu bresaola

For maximum flavour in this simple tapas dish, it's important to use good-quality blood sausages. You can buy these from good butchers. If you aren't able to get fresh padrón peppers, use tinned Spanish piquillo peppers instead.

Blood sausage with pipis, romesco & padrón peppers

SERVES 6

100 ml (3½ fl oz) extra virgin olive oil
2 blood sausages
140 g (5 oz) padrón peppers
½ bunch flat-leaf (Italian) parsley,
    leaves only
200 g (7 oz) pipis or small cockles
200 g (7 oz) clams (vongole)
splash of sherry vinegar
¼ bunch coriander (cilantro),
    leaves only
juice of 1 lemon
125 ml (4 fl oz/½ cup) Romesco sauce
    (page 231) at room temperature
crusty bread, to serve

Heat the olive oil in a frying pan over medium heat. Cut the sausages into fifths and add to the pan when the oil is hot. Cook for 30 seconds on each side. Remove from the oil and drain on paper towel.

Add the peppers to the pan and cook for 1 minute, then add the parsley and cook for another 30 seconds, stirring.

Now add the pipis, clams and vinegar. Cover with a lid and cook for a few minutes, until the pipis just start to open.

Remove from the heat and add the blood sausage back in, along with the coriander and lemon juice. Season with salt and pepper.

Serve with dollops of the romesco sauce on top, and crusty bread on the side.

Like the merguez sausages on page 162, this recipe is one of the more challenging in this book. You'll need to have the right equipment, but you'll be rewarded with the tastiest sausages. Chorizo has such a rich, smoky flavour and deep red colour from the paprika and can be used in a multitude of dishes, from paellas to pastas — as well as the frittata on page 17 and the grilled octopus recipe on page 129.

Homemade chorizos

MAKES ABOUT EIGHT 100 G (3½ OZ) SAUSAGES

sausage casings, about 1 metre (3 feet) long

SAUSAGE MIXTURE
500 g (1 lb 2 oz) pork shoulder
225 g (8 oz) pork back fat
pinch of white pepper
1 teaspoon ground cumin
2 tablespoons full-cream milk powder
1 dried red chilli
1½ red capsicums (peppers), chargrilled,
    seeded, skin removed, flesh chopped
1 tablespoon sweet paprika
1½ tablespoons smoked paprika
1½ garlic cloves, crushed

FOR THE SAUSAGES Chill a bowl and your sausage stuffer. Set a meat grinder to a very coarse setting.

Working quickly, push the pork and pork fat though the grinder, letting it fall into the chilled bowl. Place in the freezer while cleaning your grinder and work area.

Remove the pork mixture from the freezer and add the remaining sausage ingredients. Using the paddle attachment on an electric stand mixer (or a stout wooden spoon, or your VERY clean hands), mix well. Put the mixture back in the freezer while you clean up your grinder and work area again.

Run warm water through your sausage casings. This makes it easier to put them on the stuffer tube, and lets you know if there are any holes in the casings.

Fill a bowl with warm water and add the sausage casings, keeping the bowl close to the stuffer tube. Slip a casing onto the stuffer tube, leaving a 'tail' of at least 15 cm (6 inches) hanging over the end of the tube. You will need this to tie off later.

Put the sausage mixture into the stuffer. If all the mixture will not fit at once, keep it in a bowl over another bowl filled with ice, or in the fridge while you stuff the sausages in batches.

Start cranking the stuffer down. Air should be the first thing that emerges — this is why you do not tie off the casing end. When the meat starts to come out, use one hand to regulate how fast the casing slips off the tube. Let the sausage come out in one long coil; you will make links later. Leave 15–25 cm (6–10 inches) of 'tail' at the other end of the casing.

When the sausage mixture is all in the casings, tie one end in a double knot (or you could also use fine butcher's twine). With two hands, pinch off what will become two links; each link should be about 8 cm (3¼ inches) long. Work the links so they are pretty tight — you want to force any air bubbles to the end of the sausage. Now spin the link you have between your fingers away from you several times. Repeat this process down the coil, only on this next link, spin it towards you several times. Continue this way, alternating, until you get to the end of the coil. Tie off the other end.

Leave your sausages in the fridge for 6 days to cure before using. (You can either hang them in the fridge, or put them on a rack over a tray in the fridge and just leave them uncovered so the air can circulate around them.)

To cook your sausages, heat a barbecue or frying pan to medium–low heat. Do not prick the sausages, but instead cook them in a splash of oil, turning every minute until cooked through and a little charred on the outside.

Try these deliciously sticky ribs with sweet potato fries (page 64) or crumbed parsnip (page 67). Beef or lamb ribs also work well here, instead of pork. You'll find hickory liquid or liquid smoke in fine food stores.

Glazed pork spare ribs

SERVES 4

FOR THE BARBECUE SAUCE Combine all the ingredients in a bowl, mixing well. Cover and refrigerate for 24 hours. Remove the lime leaves before using.

FOR THE RIBS Place the ribs on a tray. Combine all the spices for the spice rub and rub the mixture all over the pork. Cover and refrigerate for 24 hours.

Preheat the oven to 170°C (325°F).

Place the ribs in a roasting tin, add the barbecue sauce and massage it into the ribs to coat them evenly.

Cover with a double layer of foil. Bake for 1½ hours, then leave to cool for 20 minutes. Remove the foil and refrigerate overnight.

TO SERVE Heat a barbecue to high. Place the ribs on top and cook for 5–7 minutes on each side, until glazed and caramelised.

Transfer the ribs to a serving platter, scatter with the coriander leaves and serve with the lime halves.

600 g (1 lb 5 oz) pork ribs, cut in half widthways by your butcher
¼ bunch coriander (cilantro), leaves picked
2 limes, halved

BARBECUE SAUCE
25 g (1 oz) lime leaves
250 ml (9 fl oz/1 cup) tomato sauce (ketchup)
2½ tablespoons soy sauce
2 teaspoons Tabasco or other hot sauce
2 teaspoons hickory liquid or hickory liquid smoke
100 g (3½ oz/½ cup) soft brown sugar

SPICE RUB
1 tablespoon ground cumin
1 tablespoon plus 1 teaspoon ground ginger
1 tablespoon ground coriander
1½ teaspoons ground star anise
2 teaspoons sumac
1 teaspoon ground black pepper
1 teaspoon ground cloves
1 teaspoon ground cinnamon
1 tablespoon plus 1 teaspoon garlic powder
2 tablespoons sweet paprika
1 tablespoon plus 1 teaspoon smoked paprika

Lamb neck can be substituted with diced lamb shoulder. When in season, use fresh jackfruit in the curry rather than tinned, for the best tropical flavour. You could follow this heavier style of dish with a refreshing coconut panna cotta (page 217).

Lamb neck adobo with coconut jackfruit curry & banana salsa

SERVES 4

¼ bunch coriander (cilantro), leaves only
steamed white rice, to serve

LAMB NECK ADOBO
3 teaspoons extra virgin olive oil
500 g (1 lb 2 oz) lamb neck, trimmed and
    cut into 8 cm (3¼ inch) pieces
4 garlic cloves
3 bay leaves
2 star anise, broken into pieces
1½ cinnamon sticks, broken into pieces
2 teaspoons black peppercorns
300 ml (10½ fl oz) soy sauce
3 tablespoons black vinegar
500 ml (17 fl oz/2 cups) chicken stock,
    approximately

COCONUT JACKFRUIT CURRY
extra virgin olive oil, for pan-frying
50 g (1¾ oz) French shallots, finely sliced
1 tablespoon dried shrimp, rehydrated for
    20 minutes in warm water
1½ tablespoons curry powder
440 g (15½ oz) jackfruit (tinned or fresh),
    roughly chopped
500 ml (17 fl oz/2 cups) coconut cream

BANANA SALSA
2 bananas
50 g (1¾ oz) French shallots, finely sliced
2 cm (¾ inch) piece of fresh ginger, peeled
    and grated
1 mild red chilli, chopped
1 tablespoon white vinegar
½ bunch coriander (cilantro), leaves only,
    chopped
2½ tablespoons extra virgin olive oil

FOR THE LAMB NECK ADOBO Preheat the oven to 170°C (325°F).

Heat the olive oil in a heavy-based flameproof casserole dish over medium–high heat. Add the lamb and fry for 5 minutes, or until well coloured on all sides. Add the garlic, bay leaves and spices. Stir in the soy sauce, vinegar and enough chicken stock to cover the lamb.

Cover and bake for 1–1½ hours, or until the lamb is tender, checking after 1 hour.

FOR THE COCONUT JACKFRUIT CURRY Heat a splash of olive oil in a saucepan over medium heat. Add the shallot and soaked shrimp and cook for 3–5 minutes, then stir in the curry powder and fry for 2 minutes, taking care not to let it burn.

Add the jackfruit and cook for a further 2–3 minutes, then stir in the coconut cream. Cook for 10 minutes, until the mixture has thickened. Remove from the heat and keep warm.

FOR THE BANANA SALSA Near serving time, peel the bananas and mash in a bowl. Add the remaining ingredients and mix well.

TO SERVE Place the lamb in a serving dish with the braising liquid. Sprinkle with the coriander leaves. Serve the coconut jackfruit curry, banana salsa and a little steamed rice in small dishes to accompany.

Lamb neck adobo with coconut jackfruit curry & banana salsa (page 156)

This is a really quick and fun hot dog recipe for grown-ups. The kimchi gives the dogs a good kick of spice and is best served at room temperature.

Mini hot dogs with kimchi, American mustard & chipotle mayo

MAKES 8 MINI HOTDOGS

8 mini beef hot dogs or gourmet
    frankfurters
8 mini hot dog rolls
200 g (7 oz) kimchi, chopped
    (good-quality store bought is fine,
    or see the recipe on page 225)
good-quality American mustard,
    for drizzling
Chipotle mayonnaise (page 226),
    for drizzling
120 g (4¼ oz) red cheddar cheese,
    grated (optional)
baby coriander (cilantro), to serve

Preheat the oven to 160°C (315°F).

Cook the hot dogs in a pot of simmering water for 3 minutes. Do not allow the water to boil, as boiling will break the skin.

While the hot dogs are simmering, place the hot dog buns in the oven for 2 minutes to warm them.

Gently warm the kimchi in a small saucepan.

TO SERVE Split each hot dog roll in half. Place a small amount of kimchi on the bottom half of each roll. Top with a hot dog and more kimchi.

Drizzle with mustard and chipotle mayo, then sprinkle with grated cheese, if using. Add some coriander, top with the bun lids and serve.

Flavoured with a North African spice mix, these sausages are incredibly 'moorish'. Cut the cooked sausages into slices and serve as a tapas-style dish with oysters and a cold beer. You can buy sausage casings from good butchers.

Homemade merguez sausages

sausage casings, about 1 metre (3 feet) long

MERGUEZ SPICE MIX
3 tablespoons sweet paprika
1 tablespoon ground fennel seeds
1 tablespoon ground cumin
2 teaspoons ground coriander
½ teaspoon ground cinnamon
½ teaspoon cayenne pepper
½ teaspoon freshly ground black pepper
1 tablespoon sea salt
2 teaspoons caster (superfine) sugar

SAUSAGE MIXTURE
500 g (1 lb 2 oz) boned lamb shoulder, diced
120 g (4¼ oz) pork fat, chopped
3 garlic cloves, finely chopped
2 tablespoons finely chopped coriander (cilantro)
2 tablespoons Merguez spice mix (see left)
3 teaspoons harissa
1 tablespoon sea salt

FOR THE SPICE MIX Combine all the ingredients in a bowl. Reserve 2 tablespoons of the spice mix for the sausages, and store the rest in a clean airtight jar in the pantry to use in other dishes.

FOR THE SAUSAGES Chill a bowl and your sausage stuffer. Set a meat grinder to a very coarse setting.

Working quickly, push the lamb and pork fat though the grinder, letting it fall into the chilled bowl. Place in the freezer while cleaning your grinder and work area.

Remove the lamb mixture from the freezer and add the remaining sausage ingredients. Using the paddle attachment on an electric stand mixer (or a stout wooden spoon, or your VERY clean hands), mix well. Put the mixture back in the freezer while you clean up your grinder and work area again.

Run warm water through your sausage casings. This makes it easier to put them on the stuffer tube, and lets you know if there are any holes in the casings.

Fill a bowl with warm water and add the sausage casings, keeping the bowl close to the stuffer tube. Slip a casing onto the stuffer tube, leaving a 'tail' of at least 15 cm (6 inches) hanging over the end of the tube. You will need this to tie off later.

Put the sausage mixture into the stuffer. If all the mixture will not fit at once, keep it in a bowl over another bowl filled with ice, or in the fridge while you stuff the sausages in batches.

Start cranking the stuffer down. Air should be the first thing that emerges — this is why you do not tie off the casing end. When the meat starts to come out, use one hand to regulate how fast the casing slips off the tube. Let the sausage come out in one long coil; you will make links later. Leave 15–25 cm (6–10 inches) of 'tail' at the other end of the casing.

When the sausage mixture is all in the casings, tie one end in a double knot (or you could also use fine butcher's twine). With two hands, pinch off what will become two links; each link should be about 8 cm (3¼ inches) long. Work the links so they are pretty tight — you want to force any air bubbles to the end of the sausage. Now spin the link you have between your fingers away from you several times. Repeat this process down the coil, only on this next link, spin it towards you several times. Continue this way, alternating, until you get to the end of the coil. Tie off the other end.

Leave your sausages in the fridge for 6 days to cure before using. (You can either hang them in the fridge, or put them on a rack over a tray in the fridge and just leave them uncovered so the air can circulate around them.)

To cook your sausages, heat a barbecue or frying pan to medium–low heat. Do not prick the sausages, but instead cook them in a splash of oil, turning every minute until cooked through and a little charred on the outside.

If you like a little bit of spice, add some fresh chopped chilli to the tomato sauce.

Sumac-spiced pork & veal meatballs with fontina mash

SERVES 4

FOR THE MEATBALLS Combine the veal, pork, bacon and pork fat in a large mixing bowl.

Transfer one-quarter of the meat mixture to a food processor. Add the remaining meatball ingredients and process until well combined.

Transfer the mixture to the bowl of an electric stand mixer. Add the remaining meat mixture and mix at a slow speed until the ingredients are completely combined. (Alternatively, you can do this by hand.)

Refrigerate the mixture until ready to use.

FOR THE TOMATO SAUCE Add the olive oil, shallot and garlic to a frying pan over medium heat and cook for 4–5 minutes, until softened but not coloured.

Add the paprika and the anchovies and cook for 1 minute. Deglaze the pan with the vermouth, stirring well, and cook until all the liquid has evaporated.

Stir in the tomatoes and continue to cook for 5–10 minutes, until thick. Remove from the heat and keep warm, or gently reheat for serving.

TO SERVE Divide the meatball mixture evenly into 20 pieces and roll into balls.

Add the meatballs to the warm tomato sauce and cook slowly over low heat for 12–15 minutes, or until cooked through.

Divide the fontina mash among shallow serving bowls, then top with the meatballs and tomato sauce. Sprinkle with the grated parmesan, garnish with the basil and serve hot.

½ quantity Fontina mash (page 228)
80 g (2¾ oz/¾ cup) grated parmesan
12 large basil leaves

MEATBALLS
200 g (7 oz) minced (ground) veal
180 g (6 oz) minced (ground) pork
25 g (1 oz) smoked bacon, very finely chopped or minced
50 g (1¾ oz) pork back fat, very finely chopped or minced
½ onion, very finely chopped
3 garlic cloves, crushed
2 teaspoons ground coriander
2 teaspoons sumac
2 teaspoons sea salt
⅓ teaspoon ground black pepper
⅓ teaspoon smoked paprika
½ teaspoon sweet paprika
⅓ teaspoon ground allspice
3 tablespoons milk
100 g (3½ oz) toasted fresh breadcrumbs, cooked in 3 tablespoons clarified butter

TOMATO SAUCE
80 ml (2½ fl oz/⅓ cup) extra virgin olive oil
150 g (5½ oz) French shallots, diced
2 garlic cloves, finely chopped
1 tablespoon smoked paprika
30 g (1 oz) anchovies
2½ tablespoons dry vermouth
800 g (1 lb 12 oz) tin tomatoes, chopped

If possible, buy grass-fed burger meat for these sliders, as you will really taste the difference in quality. You'll find milk buns in Asian bread shops.

Grass-fed beef sliders

MAKES 4 SLIDERS

200 g (7 oz) grass-fed minced (ground) beef
4 mini milk burger buns
extra virgin olive oil, for pan-frying
2 slices gruyère cheese, cut in half
2 bacon rashers, rind removed
2 tablespoons whole-egg mayonnaise
2 cos (romaine) lettuce leaves, cut in half to fit the burgers
2 tablespoons Onion confit (page 230)
4 thin dill pickle (gherkin) slices
good-quality barbecue sauce, for drizzling

Preheat the oven to 180°C (350°F). Preheat the grill (broiler) to medium–high.

Divide the beef into four equal portions and shape each one into a patty, flattening them to the same size as your burger buns.

Heat a drizzle of olive oil in a frying pan over medium heat. Add the patties to the pan, season with salt and pepper, and cook on one side for 2 minutes. Turn the patties over, place the cheese slices on top and cook for a further 2 minutes. Remove from the pan and leave to rest for 2 minutes.

Meanwhile, warm the burger buns in the oven for 3 minutes, and cook the bacon rashers under the grill.

TO SERVE Cut the warm burger buns in half widthways. Cut the bacon rashers in half.

Spread the mayonnaise on the base of each bun. Top with a piece of lettuce, then a burger patty. Add a dollop of onion confit, a bacon slice and dill pickle. Drizzle with barbecue sauce and top with the other half of the bun.

Chapter 7
Poultry

I love sharing food at the table; tapas and shared plates are such a social way of eating.

More often than not people don't always want to do the three-course meal for dinner parties anymore, but rather offer one beautiful dish or a couple of little dishes in the middle of the table for guests to share and help themselves to.

This chapter has a mix of more challenging yet really satisfying recipes such as duck prosciutto with sliced pear, toasted walnuts and elderflower dressing (page 173) and a rustic chicken pâté with pear and shallot dressing (page 175), to simple weeknight meals of chicken garam masala with raita (page 174) and tandoori roasted drumsticks with cucumber, chilli and coriander salad (page 180).

There are also some great small bites and party-type fare, such as mini chicken katsu sandwiches with shaved cabbage (page 185) and baked spicy chicken drumettes with romesco (page 170).

These little chicken drumettes are about as easy and flavoursome as they come. Marinate them overnight if you have time, to really get the most out of the spices. I can't tell you how many times we're asked for this recipe. It never fails.

Baked spicy chicken drumettes with romesco

SERVES 4–6

12 chicken drumettes
80 ml (2½ fl oz/⅓ cup) vegetable oil
chicken salt, to taste
250 ml (9 fl oz/1 cup) Romesco sauce
   (page 231)
¼ bunch coriander (cilantro),
   to garnish

CHICKEN SPICE MIX
35 g (1¼ oz/¼ cup) plain
   (all-purpose) flour
1½ teaspoons sea salt
1 teaspoon freshly ground black
   pepper
1½ tablespoons sweet paprika
1½ tablespoons smoked paprika
1½ tablespoons curry powder
2 tablespoons dried oregano leaves

Combine the chicken spice mix ingredients in a large food bag. Add the chicken to the flour mixture, shaking to ensure the drumettes are evenly coated. Refrigerate for at least 2 hours, or overnight.

TO SERVE Preheat the oven to 170°C (325°F). Line a baking tray with baking paper.
   Arrange the chicken on the baking tray and drizzle with the vegetable oil. Bake for 25–30 minutes, turning every 5 minutes. Drain on paper towel, then season with chicken salt.
   Dollop the romesco sauce onto a large serving plate. Arrange the warm chicken on top. Garnish with the coriander and serve.

Making your own prosciutto is really quite satisfying — I encourage you to give it a go. When peaches are not in season, pears or apples work just as well in this tapas dish: the fruit cuts through the fat of the prosciutto so beautifully.

Duck prosciutto with sliced peach, toasted walnuts & elderflower dressing

SERVES 6

FOR THE DUCK PROSCIUTTO Rinse the duck breasts in cold water and pat dry with paper towel.

In a bowl, mix together the garlic, thyme, rosemary and salt. Spread half the mixture on a tray. Place the duck breasts on top, then cover with the remaining herbed salt. Cover with plastic wrap and refrigerate for 24 hours.

The next day, lightly toast the coriander seeds, fennel seeds and black pepper in a small dry frying pan over medium heat for about 1 minute, or until they smell fragrant, stirring frequently so they don't burn. Grind to a powder using a mortar and pestle, or a small spice grinder. Tip the spices into a bowl and mix the chilli flakes through.

Rinse the duck breasts with cold water, then wash with the vinegar. Rinse with water again, then dry thoroughly with paper towel.

Rub the spice mixture all over the duck breasts. Individually wrap them in muslin (cheesecloth), tying a knot in the cloth at both ends. Tie one end with kitchen string and hang in the fridge for up to 2 weeks. (If you can't hang them, put them on a rack over a tray and leave uncovered in the fridge, so the air can circulate.) Check smaller breasts after 1 week as they will take less time to cure, and you don't want the meat too hard.

FOR THE DRESSING Place all the ingredients in a jar, screw the lid on and shake well.

TO SERVE Use a sharp knife to slice the duck prosciutto as thinly as possible, preferably paper thin. Arrange on serving plates. Scatter the peaches, walnuts and salad leaves around. Drizzle with the dressing and serve.

2 peaches, stoned, cut into 6 wedges each
60 g (2¼ oz/½ cup) walnuts, toasted
100 g (3½ oz) mixed baby salad leaves

DUCK PROSCIUTTO
6 duck breasts
3–4 garlic cloves, crushed
2 thyme sprigs, leaves picked
3 rosemary sprigs, leaves picked
170 g (5¾ oz) table salt
1 tablespoon plus 1 teaspoon coriander seeds
1 tablespoon plus 1 teaspoon fennel seeds
1 tablespoon plus 1 teaspoon black peppercorns
2 teaspoons chilli flakes
170 ml (5½ fl oz/⅔ cup) white wine vinegar

ELDERFLOWER DRESSING
150 ml (5 fl oz) apple cider vinegar
65 ml (2 fl oz) elderflower cordial
125 ml (4 fl oz/½ cup) extra virgin olive oil

Garam masala is a beautiful blend of aromatic spices and tastes so much fresher when you make your own. This light summer meal is perfect with a refreshing glass of lassi, and the spinach parathas on page 49.

Chicken garam masala with raita & tomato & onion salad

SERVES 6

6 boneless chicken thighs, skin on
extra virgin olive oil, for drizzling

GARAM MASALA
16 green cardamom pods, crushed,
    reserving the seeds
2 bay leaves, torn into small bits
2 teaspoons black peppercorns
4 teaspoons cumin seeds
2 teaspoons coriander seeds
2 cinnamon sticks, broken up roughly
½ teaspoon cloves

MINT & CORIANDER RAITA
100 g (3½ oz) plain yoghurt
1 Lebanese (short) cucumber,
    seeded and finely diced
1 tablespoon lime juice
¼ bunch mint
¼ bunch coriander (cilantro)

TOMATO & ONION SALAD
2 teaspoons yellow mustard seeds
½ red onion, thinly sliced
3 tomatoes, cut into 2.5 cm (1 inch) dice
¼ bunch coriander (cilantro), leaves
    only, roughly torn
¼ bunch mint, leaves only, roughly torn
3 tablespoons Crisp shallots & garlic
    (page 227)
1½ tablespoons fish sauce
2 tablespoons lime juice
2½ tablespoons extra virgin olive oil

FOR THE CHICKEN Using a spice grinder or mortar and pestle, grind all the garam masala spices to a fine powder.

Rub the chicken with a little olive oil, then coat the chicken in the garam masala and season with salt and pepper. Transfer the chicken to a bowl, cover and refrigerate for 2–3 hours.

When nearly ready to serve, preheat the oven to 180°C (350°F).

Place the chicken on a rack over a baking tray and bake for 25–30 minutes, until cooked through.

FOR THE RAITA While the chicken is baking, combine the yoghurt, cucumber and lime juice in a bowl. Pick the leaves from the mint and coriander and chop them. Mix them through the raita and set aside.

FOR THE SALAD Place the mustard seeds in a dry frying pan and lightly toast over medium–low heat until they begin to pop.

Transfer to a bowl and combine with the remaining ingredients. Mix well.

TO SERVE Place the warm baked chicken on a small platter, serving the raita and salad alongside.

This rather gutsy pâté makes a perfect shared starter. Truffle paste is available from fine food stores; if it proves elusive, you could use a tablespoon of truffle oil instead.

Rustic chicken pâté with pear & shallot relish

SERVES 4–6

FOR THE PEAR & SHALLOT RELISH Place all the ingredients in a saucepan over medium heat and bring to a simmer. Cook for 45 minutes, stirring now and then, until the mixture has a thick consistency. Remove from the heat and leave to cool. Transfer the relish to an airtight container and refrigerate for 2 days before use. This will keep in the fridge for 3 weeks, but bring it to room temperature for serving.

FOR THE PATE Heat 40 g (1½ oz) of the butter in a saucepan over medium–high heat. Add the chicken livers and bacon and cook for 1–2 minutes; the livers should still be pink in the middle. Add the Cognac and carefully set the pan alight to flambé the livers. Pour the mixture onto a tray and place in the fridge to cool quickly.

In a clean saucepan, heat a splash of olive oil over medium heat. Add the onion and garlic and cook for 3–4 minutes, until soft. Stir in the port, wine and herbs and continue to cook for 10–12 minutes, until reduced to a thick syrup.

Remove the herbs and transfer the reduction to a food processor. Add the chicken liver mixture and blend roughly. Add the remaining butter and the truffle paste and continue blending until the mixture is smooth and the butter well incorporated. Season with salt and pepper.

Place in a container and refrigerate for 3–4 hours.

TO SERVE Drizzle the watercress with olive oil and cabernet sauvignon vinegar. Place a generous spoonful of pâté on each serving plate, with some relish and watercress. Serve with toasted thinly sliced bread.

handful watercress leaves
extra virgin olive oil, for drizzling
Cabernet sauvignon dressing
   (page 226), for drizzling
thin bread toasts, to serve

PEAR & SHALLOT RELISH
625 g (1 lb 6 oz) French shallots,
   thinly sliced
375 g (13 oz) pears, cored and diced
3 cm (1¼ inch) piece of fresh ginger,
   peeled and finely grated
60 g (2¼ oz/⅓ cup) raisins
pinch of ground cinnamon
2 teaspoons brown mustard seeds
pinch of mustard powder
250 ml (9 fl oz/1 cup) apple cider
   vinegar
150 g (5½ oz/¾ cup) soft brown sugar

CHICKEN PATE
200 g (7 oz) unsalted butter
250 g (9 oz) chicken livers, trimmed
150 g (5½ oz) bacon, finely chopped
100 ml (3½ fl oz) Cognac
extra virgin olive oil, for pan-frying
½ onion, finely chopped
2 garlic cloves, finely chopped
200 ml (7 fl oz) port
200 ml (7 fl oz) red wine
6 thyme sprigs
2 sage sprigs
40 g (1½ oz) truffle paste

Tandoori-roasted drumsticks with cucumber, chilli & coriander salad (page 180)

Southern-style quail with buttermilk dressing & cucumber pickle (page 178)

Rustic chicken pâté with pear & shallot relish (page 175)

Chicken garam masala with raita & tomato & onion salad (page 174)

Sweet potato fries (page 64) are an irresistible accompaniment to this tasty sharing dish. Instead of quail, you could also use boneless chicken thighs, with the skin still on. The buttermilk dressing is perfect tossed through salads, drizzled over fish, or as a dipping sauce for fresh seafood.

Southern-style quail with buttermilk dressing & cucumber pickle

SERVES 6

CUCUMBER PICKLE
½ onion, sliced
½ green capsicum (pepper), sliced
6 teaspoons fine sea salt
300 g (10½ oz) Lebanese (short) cucumbers
150 ml (5 fl oz) white wine vinegar
¼ teaspoon ground turmeric
⅓ teaspoon ground cloves
3 teaspoons yellow mustard seeds
1 teaspoon celery seeds
120 g (4¼ oz) soft brown sugar

BUTTERMILK DRESSING
75 g (2½ oz/¼ cup) mayonnaise
100 ml (3½ fl oz) buttermilk
75 g (2½ oz/½ cup) plain yoghurt
3 teaspoons lemon juice
15 g (½ oz) Garlic confit (page 229)
1 teaspoon dijon mustard

SOUTHERN-STYLE QUAIL
3 quails
200 ml (7 fl oz) buttermilk
2 free-range eggs
80 ml (2½ fl oz/⅓ cup) Louisiana hot sauce
250 g (9 oz/1⅔ cups) self-raising flour
1 tablespoon celery salt
1 tablespoon onion powder
1 tablespoon garlic powder
1 tablespoon hot paprika
1 tablespoon sea salt
3 teaspoons freshly ground black pepper
vegetable oil, for deep-frying

FOR THE CUCUMBER PICKLE In a bowl, toss together the onion, capsicum and 3 teaspoons of the salt. Set aside for 3 hours, then wash in water and drain well.

Peel the cucumbers and cut in half lengthways; remove the seeds and slice the flesh. Sprinkle with the remaining 3 teaspoons of salt and set aside for 10 minutes. Rinse the salt off and place the cucumber in the fridge.

Combine the vinegar and spices in a saucepan and bring to the boil. Add the brown sugar and bring to the boil again. Remove from the heat and set aside to cool.

In a clean airtight container, combine the cucumber, onion and capsicum. Pour the cooled pickling liquid over, then seal and refrigerate for at least 2 days.

The pickle will keep in the fridge for up to 1 month.

FOR THE BUTTERMILK DRESSING Whisk all the ingredients together, season with salt and pepper, and chill for several hours before using.

FOR THE QUAIL Place the quails on a chopping board and cut into quarters. Keep the winglet on the breast and remove the thigh bone from the leg portions. (You can ask your butcher to do this for you.)

In a bowl, mix together the buttermilk, eggs and hot sauce. Add the quail, making sure all the pieces are coated. Marinate in the fridge for 45 minutes, then drain well.

In another bowl, combine the flour and all the spices. Toss the quail pieces in the mixture until evenly coated.

Reserving the spice mixture, place the quail pieces on a tray and refrigerate for 30 minutes, to allow the coating to dry so they brown perfectly.

About 10 minutes before you're ready to serve, take the quail out of the fridge to come back to room temperature.

Meanwhile, two-thirds fill a deep-fryer or large heavy-based saucepan with vegetable oil. Heat to 165°C (320°F), or until a cube of bread dropped into the oil turns golden brown in 30 seconds.

Coat the quail in the spice mixture again. Deep-fry in batches for 3–5 minutes, until golden brown and crispy all over.

Drain well on paper towel and leave to rest for 2 minutes.

TO SERVE Place the warm fried quail on a serving plate, top with the pickled cucumber and serve the buttermilk dressing on the side.

Marinating the drumsticks in spiced yoghurt makes them very tender and moist. These are simply lovely with warm spinach parathas (page 49), or garlic naan breads or wraps.

Tandoori-roasted drumsticks with cucumber, chilli & coriander salad

SERVES 4

8 chicken drumsticks
200 g (7 oz/¾ cup) plain yoghurt,
   to serve

TANDOORI MARINADE
1½ tablespoons extra virgin olive oil
200 g (7 oz/¾ cup) plain yoghurt
1 teaspoon finely chopped fresh
   ginger
1 teaspoon finely chopped garlic
1 tablespoon lime or lemon juice
1 teaspoon sweet paprika
½ teaspoon mustard powder
½ teaspoon ground cumin
¼ teaspoon chilli powder
pinch of garam masala
pinch of ground turmeric

CUCUMBER, CHILLI & CORIANDER SALAD
1 telegraph (long) cucumber, peeled
   and sliced
½ bunch coriander (cilantro), leaves
   only, roughly chopped
½ red chilli, finely chopped
juice of ½ lime
2 teaspoons fish sauce
1 tablespoon extra virgin olive oil

TO MARINATE THE CHICKEN Combine all the marinade ingredients in a bowl. Add the chicken and stir to coat. Cover and refrigerate for at least 6 hours, but no longer than 8 hours.

FOR THE SALAD Near serving time, combine all the ingredients in a bowl and mix well.

TO SERVE Heat a barbecue or chargrill pan to high.
   Remove the chicken from the marinade and place on the hotplate. Reduce the heat to medium–low and cook, turning often, for 15–20 minutes, or until the chicken is cooked through.
   Arrange the warm drumsticks on a serving platter, top with the salad and serve with the yoghurt.

This is a really simple, budget-friendly sharing dish, inspired by my Tokyo travels, sampling the most delicious chicken dishes in small yakitori bars. The recipe could easily be doubled or even tripled for a larger crowd. Serve hot out of the oven, with plenty of napkins.

Spicy soy, ginger & sesame chicken wings

MAKES 6 WINGS

FOR THE GLAZE Put all the ingredients into a small saucepan and bring to a simmer over medium heat. Stirring constantly, allow the mixture to reduce for about 6–8 minutes.

Remove from the heat and set aside.

FOR THE WINGS Preheat the oven to 180°C (350°F). Line a baking tray with baking paper.

Place the wings in a large bowl. Add the sesame oil, chicken salt, pepper and paprika and mix well to combine. Arrange the wings on a baking tray, then bake for 45 minutes, flipping them over halfway through.

Remove from the oven and drizzle half the glaze over the wings, turning until evenly coated. Return to the oven and bake for 3–4 minutes, then turn the wings over and bake for a further 3–4 minutes.

Remove the wings from the oven and toss in the remaining glaze. Sprinkle with the sesame seeds and serve.

SPICY SOY & GINGER GLAZE
100 ml (3½ fl oz) low-salt soy sauce
90 g (3¼ oz/¼ cup) plus 2 teaspoons honey
2 tablespoons finely grated fresh ginger
140 ml (4½ fl oz) hot sauce, such as sriracha
2 teaspoons sweet paprika
1 tablespoon garlic powder

CHICKEN WINGS
6 chicken wings
2 tablespoons sesame oil
2 teaspoons chicken salt
½ teaspoon freshly ground black pepper
1 teaspoon sweet paprika
3 tablespoons sesame seeds, lightly toasted

After a trip to Tokyo in 1996, I put this dish on the menu at my first restaurant. It's still a favourite today. It makes an elegant starter or shared dish at an Asian-inspired table.

Tempura quail with carrot & daikon salad & wasabi

SERVES 4

2 jumbo quails
50 g (1¾ oz) soft brown sugar
50 g (1¾ oz) rock salt
3 nori sheets
vegetable oil, for deep-frying
plain (all-purpose) flour, for dusting
1 quantity Tempura batter (page 232)
Wasabi dressing (page 233), to serve

CARROT & DAIKON SALAD
1 carrot
¼ daikon radish
30 g (1 oz) unsalted butter
50 g (1¾ oz) honey
2 tablespoons sesame seeds
¼ bunch of baby watercress

FOR THE QUAIL Place the quails on a chopping board and cut into quarters. Keep the winglet on the breast and remove the thigh bone from the leg portions. (You can ask your butcher to do this for you.)

Place the quail in a large bowl. Combine the brown sugar and rock salt and cover the quail with this mixture. Leave to cure for 15 minutes.

Brush the nori sheets with water and cut into quarters. Wrap each of the quail pieces in a piece of nori.

Two-thirds fill a deep-fryer or large heavy-based saucepan with vegetable oil. Heat to 170°C (325°F), or until a cube of bread dropped into the oil turns golden brown in 20 seconds.

Dust the quail pieces with flour, then coat in the tempura batter. Gently lower into the hot oil and cook for 1½ minutes. Remove and drain on paper towel for 2 minutes, then return to the fryer and cook for another 1 minute.

FOR THE SALAD Peel the carrot and daikon, then shave them into strips using a vegetable peeler.

Heat the butter, honey and sesame seeds in a saucepan over medium heat, until the sauce begins to froth. Add the vegetable strips and cook for 2–3 minutes to soften.

Transfer to a bowl and season with salt and pepper. Mix the watercress through the hot vegetables.

TO SERVE Slice the larger quail pieces using a sharp knife, then arrange on a platter with the salad. Serve immediately, with the wasabi dressing.

It's important to use really fresh white bread for these sandwiches. The katsu sauce will keep in an airtight container in the fridge for up to a month, and also makes a terrific dipping sauce for prawns or Japanese tonkatsu dishes. Adjust the quantities if serving more people.

Chicken katsu sandwiches with shaved cabbage salad

MAKES 4 FINGER SANDWICHES

FOR THE KATSU SAUCE Combine all the ingredients in a saucepan over medium heat and bring to the boil, stirring occasionally. Reduce the heat to low and simmer for 10–12 minutes, skimming off any foam that rises to the top.

Remove from the heat and keep warm.

FOR THE CHICKEN KATSU Cut the chicken thighs in half and place between two pieces of plastic wrap. Use a rolling pin or the side of a pan to pound them to half their original thickness.

Place the flour, eggs and panko crumbs in separate bowls.

Season the chicken with salt and pepper and dip in the flour to coat. Dip into the egg, then the crumbs.

Two-thirds fill a deep-fryer or large heavy-based saucepan with vegetable oil. Heat to 180°C (350°F), or until a cube of bread dropped into the oil turns golden brown in 15 seconds.

Add the chicken and cook for 5–6 minutes, or until golden brown and cooked all the way through. Drain on paper towel.

FOR THE CABBAGE SALAD Combine all the ingredients in a bowl and set aside.

TO SERVE Spread the bread slices with the butter and katsu sauce. Top half the slices with the chicken pieces and a little cabbage salad, then sandwich the other bread slices on top.

Cut the crusts off and cut the sandwiches in half. Serve immediately.

4 slices white bread
good-quality salted butter,
    for spreading

KATSU SAUCE
100 ml (3½ fl oz) tomato sauce
    (ketchup)
1½ tablespoons worcestershire sauce
1 tablespoon sake
1 tablespoon mirin
2 teaspoons finely chopped fresh
    ginger
2 teaspoons finely chopped garlic
1½ tablespoons caster (superfine)
    sugar

CHICKEN KATSU
2 skinless, boneless chicken thighs
70 g (2½ oz/½ cup) plain (all-
    purpose) flour
1–2 free-range eggs, beaten
60 g (2¼ oz/1 cup) panko crumbs
    (or breadcrumbs)
vegetable oil, for deep-frying

CABBAGE SALAD
75 g (2½ oz/1 cup) thinly shaved
    cabbage
1 tablespoon rice wine vinegar
2 tablespoons extra virgin olive oil

Instead of duck legs, you can use chicken legs or marylands in these cigars, to make them more cost effective. Make sure you keep the duck fat once you've finished preparing the confit — it can be used again in another confit, or for cooking the most sensational roast potatoes.

Confit duck & mustard fruit cigars with watercress & olive & capsicum jam

MAKES 8 CIGARS

½ bunch watercress, leaves picked
Cabernet sauvignon dressing (page 226), for drizzling

OLIVE & CAPSICUM JAM
6 large red capsicum (peppers)
165 g (5¾ oz/¾ cup) caster (superfine) sugar
150 ml (5 fl oz) red wine vinegar
2 red chillies, finely chopped
100 g (3½ oz) pitted black olives, roughly chopped

CONFIT DUCK
315 g (11 oz/1 cup) rock salt
1 garlic bulb, chopped (no need to peel)
½ bunch thyme
8 duck legs
2 litres (35 fl oz/8 cups) warm duck fat, approximately

DUCK & MUSTARD FRUIT CIGARS
250 ml (9 fl oz/1 cup) veal glaze (from a good deli)
200 g (7 oz) Onion confit (page 230)
150 g (5½ oz) mustard fruits, finely chopped
80 ml (2½ fl oz/⅓ cup) syrup from the mustard fruits
½ bunch tarragon, leaves only, finely chopped
8 brick pastry sheets or large spring roll wrappers
2 free-range eggs, lightly beaten with 1 tablespoon milk
vegetable oil, for shallow-frying

FOR THE JAM Finely chop the capsicums, removing the seeds and membranes. Place in a bowl, season with salt and leave to stand for 3 hours.

Tip the capsicums into a saucepan. Add the sugar, vinegar and chillies and cook over medium–low heat for 1 hour, or until a jammy consistency is reached.

Remove from the heat, add the olives, season with salt and pepper and mix well. Cover and set aside while preparing the cigars.

FOR THE CONFIT DUCK Place the rock salt, garlic and thyme in a food processor and blend until combined. Transfer to a large bowl, add the duck legs and toss until coated all over. Cover and marinate in the fridge for 2 hours.

Preheat the oven to 100°C (200°F). Rinse the duck legs and pat dry with paper towel.

Place the duck in a deep baking dish and add enough warm duck fat to cover. Bake for 2–3 hours, or until the meat is tender.

Cool slightly, then remove the duck legs from the fat with a slotted spoon, placing them on a tray to continue cooling. Pour the duck fat in an airtight container and keep in the freezer for your next meat confit, or for roasting potatoes.

FOR THE DUCK CIGARS Pour the veal glaze into a saucepan and simmer over medium heat for 10–12 minutes, until reduced by half. Set aside and keep warm.

Pick the duck meat from the bones and place into a clean bowl. Add the warm veal glaze, onion confit, chopped mustard fruits and syrup, and tarragon leaves. Mix well and season with salt and pepper.

Place the brick pastry on the bench. Add 40–50 g (1½ –1¾ oz) of the duck mixture to bottom of each pastry sheet. Brush the pastry sheets with the egg wash and bring the sides of the pastry in. Roll the pastry to form a cigar and seal the ends.

Pour about 2 cm (¾ inch) vegetable oil into a frying pan, for shallow-frying. (Alternatively you can deep-fry the cigars.) Heat the oil over medium heat to 170°C (325°F), or until a cube of bread dropped into the oil turns golden brown in 20 seconds.

Carefully place the cigars in the pan and cook for about 3–5 minutes, until golden brown, turning them every 30 seconds or so. Drain on paper towel.

TO SERVE Arrange the warm cigars on a platter. Toss the watercress with a little cabernet sauvignon dressing and use it to garnish the platter. Serve immediately, with the olive and capsicum jam.

Confit duck & mustard fruit cigars with
watercress & olive & capsicum jam
(page 186)

Tamarillo, also known as a tree tomato, is often one of those forgotten fruits, but works beautifully in this recipe. Tamarillos have a taste not dissimilar to a passionfruit and marry perfectly with the cured duck because of their wonderful acidity. I wouldn't really use any other fruit in the glaze when fresh tamarillos are not available — so when they are in season, do try to make the most of them.

Salt & sugar-cured duck breast with sichuan pepper, turnip & tamarillo glaze

SERVES 4–6

2 large duck breasts
2 tablespoons sichuan peppercorns, lightly crushed
50 g (1¾ oz) soft brown sugar
50 g (1¾ oz) rock salt
3 tamarillos
1 large turnip
daikon radish cress, to garnish

TAMARILLO GLAZE
3 tamarillos
25 g (1 oz) sichuan peppercorns, lightly crushed
3 tablespoons extra virgin olive oil
1 tablespoon chardonnay vinegar

FOR THE DUCK Trim the duck breasts of all sinew and place in a bowl. Combine the sichuan pepper, brown sugar and rock salt together and use it to coat the duck breasts. Refrigerate for 2 hours.

Preheat the oven to 180°C (350°F).

Rinse the duck breasts with cold water and pat dry with paper towel. Season the duck skin with salt and pepper.

Place the duck, skin side down, in a cold ovenproof frying pan over low heat. Leave for 8–10 minutes to render the fat.

Turn the duck breasts over, then transfer the pan to the oven for 2–3 minutes. Remove from the oven and place the duck breasts, skin side down, on a tray to rest.

FOR THE TAMARILLO GLAZE While the duck is curing in the fridge, pass the tamarillos through a juicer or blender with 100 ml (3½ fl oz) of water. Strain in a small saucepan.

Add the sichuan peppercorns and bring to a simmer. Leave to simmer for 5–8 minutes, until the liquid has reduced by half.

Strain into a bowl. Whisk in the olive oil and vinegar.

FOR THE TAMARILLO & TURNIP SLICES Near serving time, bring a small saucepan of water to the boil. Add the whole tamarillos and cook for 30–40 seconds. Remove with a slotted spoon and transfer to a bowl of cold water.

When the tamarillos have cooled, drain them, peel them, then cut each one into five slices.

Bring the saucepan of water back to the boil. Cut the turnip into slices 5 mm (¼ inch) thick. Use a pastry cutter to cut out small rounds the same size as the tamarillo slices. Add the turnips to the boiling water and cook for 40–60 seconds.

Drain and keep warm.

TO SERVE Use a sharp knife to slice the duck breasts. Layer the turnip and tamarillo slices on a serving plate and garnish with daikon radish cress.

Top with the sliced duck, drizzle with the tamarillo glaze and serve.

Chapter 8
Sweets

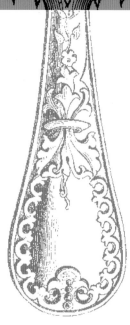

If you have a sweet tooth anything like mine, you'll love the recipes in this chapter. There are some absolutely more-ish recipes here — good, wholesome sweets and desserts without any foams or deconstructed anything.

When we were working on the menus for our first tapas restaurant in Singapore, we wanted to create a casual place for people to come in, sit at the bar, have a drink and a couple of small plates and share them with friends. Nothing fussy, just decent food. We put a gooey chocolate tart (page 196) on the menu as a special, thinking it may come and go — but we found some of our customers coming in just for this dessert! It became a permanent fixture on the menu and is still in most of our restaurants.

Admittedly, some of the desserts in this chapter, such as the pistachio and chocolate cake with braised quince (page 200) and the peanut butter ice cream sandwich with dulce de leche and cherry sorbet (page 218), do have a few steps to them, but don't let this deter you. Many of these recipes contain smaller elements that you can make in advance. And great desserts like these are always a memorable and impressive end to an otherwise simple meal.

Make these amazing bombs of honeycomb well in advance and keep them in the freezer, so you can pull them out any time that calls for a sweet little bite.

Salted chocolate honeycomb

cooking oil or spray, for greasing
125 g (4½ oz) liquid glucose
360 g (12¾ oz) caster (superfine) sugar
3 tablespoons honey
15 g (½ oz) bicarbonate of soda (baking soda)
250 g (9 oz) dark chocolate
sea salt, for sprinkling

Line a heatproof tray with baking paper and lightly oil it.

Place the glucose, sugar, honey and 75 ml (2¼ fl oz) water in a saucepan over medium heat. Stir until the sugar has dissolved, then cook until the mixture turns a quite dark caramel colour.

Remove from the heat and leave to stand for 2 minutes, before whisking in the bicarbonate of soda. Whisk just enough so that it is incorporated into the caramel, ensuring not to over-mix or the honeycomb will collapse.

Pour onto the prepared tray and leave at room temperature for about 1 hour to cool.

Once the honeycomb has set, break it into bite-sized pieces. Set a wire rack over a tray.

Melt the chocolate in a heatproof bowl set over a saucepan of simmering water. Remove from the heat, dip the honeycomb bits into the melted chocolate, and place on the wire rack.

Sprinkle with sea salt and allow the chocolate to set. Store in the freezer until required.

This is one of our signature desserts, which we can't take off our menu. If you don't have enough time to make all the components, take a shortcut by buying a good-quality caramel ice cream, instead of making your own.

Gooey chocolate tarts with caramelised banana & caramel ice cream

CARAMEL ICE CREAM
395 g (13¾ oz) tin of sweetened
    condensed milk
500 ml (17 fl oz/2 cups) milk
2 tablespoons lime juice
500 g (1 lb 2 oz) liquid glucose

HONEYCOMB
cooking oil or spray
125 g (4½ oz) liquid glucose
360 g (12¾ oz) caster (superfine) sugar
3 tablespoons honey
2 teaspoons bicarbonate of soda
    (baking soda)

CHOCOLATE SWEET PASTRY
1 free-range egg
1 free-range egg yolk
70 g (2½ oz) icing (confectioners') sugar
125 g (4½ oz) unsalted butter, at room
    temperature
150 g (5½ oz/1 cup) plain (all-purpose) flour,
    plus extra for dusting
40 g (1½ oz/⅓ cup) unsweetened cocoa
    powder

CHOCOLATE TART FILLING
95 g (3¼ oz) dark chocolate (72% cocoa)
90 g (3¼ oz) unsalted butter, chopped
3 free-range eggs
150 g (5½ oz/⅔ cup) caster (superfine) sugar
55 g (2 oz) plain (all-purpose) flour, sifted

CARAMELISED BANANA
4 baby or lady finger bananas, skin on,
    cut in half lengthways
4 tablespoons soft brown sugar

FOR THE CARAMEL ICE CREAM Remove the label from the unopened tin of condensed milk. Fill a deep, medium-sized saucepan with water and bring to the boil. Carefully place the tin in the saucepan, ensuring there is enough water to completely cover the tin at all times. Simmer, uncovered, for 3 hours, topping up the water frequently. Carefully remove the tin from the boiling water. Allow to cool completely before opening.

Warm the milk in a saucepan over medium heat. Add the caramel from the condensed milk tin, whisking well to ensure there are no lumps. Remove from the heat, add the lime juice and glucose and mix well. Strain into a bowl and chill for 2–3 hours until cold.

Pour into an ice cream maker. Churn until just set, then transfer to an airtight container and place in the freezer until needed.

FOR THE HONEYCOMB Line a 20 x 30 cm (8 x 12 inch) heatproof tray with baking paper and lightly oil it. Place the glucose, sugar, honey and 75 ml (2¼ fl oz) water in a saucepan over medium heat. Stir until the sugar has dissolved, then cook until the mixture turns quite a dark caramel colour.

Remove from the heat, stand for 2 minutes, then whisk in the bicarbonate of soda. Whisk just enough so that it is incorporated into the caramel, taking care not to over-mix or the honeycomb will collapse.

Pour onto the prepared tray and leave at room temperature for about 1 hour to cool. Break into pieces when set. Store in the freezer in an airtight container until needed.

FOR THE PASTRY In the bowl of an electric stand mixer, whisk the egg, egg yolk and icing sugar for 3–4 minutes, until pale and thick. Change from the whisk to a paddle attachment, if your mixer has one, then slowly add the butter and mix until combined.

Sift the flour and cocoa powder together and lightly fold into the egg mixture, scraping down the side of the bowl to ensure it is well combined. Turn onto a lightly floured surface and gently knead until almost smooth. Shape into a disc, cover with plastic wrap and rest in the fridge for 30 minutes.

Preheat the oven to 165°C (320°F). Set out eight 9 cm (3½ inch) round, fluted tart (flan) tins with removable bases. On a lightly floured surface, roll the dough out 4 mm (³⁄₁₆ inch) thick. Cut into eight 12 cm (4½ inch) circles. Line the tart tins, trim the edges with a sharp knife and rest in the fridge for 15 minutes.

Place the tart tins on a baking tray. Line the pastry with baking paper and fill with dried rice or beans. Bake for 10 minutes, then remove the baking paper and rice or beans and bake for a further 5 minutes, or until pastry is just cooked through. Remove from the heat and leave to cool.

FOR THE FILLING Place the chocolate and butter in a metal bowl and set over a saucepan of simmering water until melted.

Whisk the eggs and sugar together in a bowl until light and pale. Add the melted chocolate mixture and stir to combine. Fold the sifted flour through.

TO BAKE THE TARTS Preheat the oven to 170°C (325°F). Place the tart shells on a baking tray. Spoon the chocolate tart filling into a piping (icing) bag and pipe into each tart case.

Bake for 6–7 minutes, until the filling is just set, but still gooey inside.

FOR THE CARAMELISED BANANA While the tarts are in the oven, place the bananas on a heatproof tray and sprinkle with the sugar.

Use a kitchen blow torch to melt the sugar until you have a nice caramel, or place the coated bananas under a hot grill (broiler).

TO SERVE Top each tart with some bits of honeycomb. Serve with the caramelised banana and a scoop of caramel ice cream.

Gooey chocolate tart with caramelised banana & caramel ice cream (page 196)

Pistachio & chocolate cake with
red wine & coffee-braised quince (page 200)

*Ambrosial quince, soaked in red wine and aromatic spices, makes this dessert
a pure delight. Admittedly, there are a few different components to this cake,
but all the flavours work so well together. When quince is out of season,
you can use pears, but the flavour won't be quite as special.*

Pistachio & chocolate cake with red wine & coffee-braised quince

SERVES 8–12

RED WINE & COFFEE-BRAISED QUINCE
2 quinces
1½ cinnamon sticks
3 cloves
3 whole allspice berries
1 tablespoon coffee beans
1 litre (35 fl oz/4 cups) red wine
350 g (12 oz) caster (superfine) sugar
peel and juice of 2 oranges

CHOCOLATE SPONGE
5 free-range eggs
100 g (3½ oz) caster (superfine) sugar
35 g (1¼ oz) plain (all-purpose) flour, sifted
1 tablespoon unsweetened cocoa powder

PISTACHIO GANACHE
35 g (1¼ oz) milk chocolate, coarsely
    chopped
35 ml (1¼ fl oz) pouring (single) cream
50 g (1¾ oz) pistachio paste

PISTACHIO MOUSSE
115 g (4 oz) milk chocolate
1 free-range egg
3 free-range egg yolks
95 g (3¼ oz) caster (superfine) sugar
3 gelatine sheets (gold-strength), soaked in
    cold water for 5 minutes
1 quantity pistachio ganache (see left)
250 ml (9 fl oz/1 cup) pouring (single) cream,
    whipped to soft peaks
cooking oil or spray, for greasing

TO GARNISH
8 basil leaves, thinly sliced

TO BRAISE THE QUINCES Preheat the oven to 160°C (315°F). Peel the quinces, reserving the skin. Cut in half and place in a roasting tin. Wrap the skins in a piece of cheesecloth (muslin) and tie securely with kitchen string. Seal up the spices and coffee beans in another cloth bundle.

Place the bag of quince skins and the spice bag in a saucepan. Add the wine, sugar, and the orange peel and juice. Pour in 500 ml (17 fl oz/2 cups) water and bring to a simmer over medium–high heat.

Pour the mixture (including the spice bags) over the quinces in the roasting tin. Cover with foil and bake for 40 minutes, or until the quince is tender but not mushy; this may take up to 1 hour. Remove the foil and leave the quince to cool in the liquid.

Transfer the cooled quince pieces to a bowl, discarding the spice and quince-skin bags. Place the braising liquid in a saucepan over medium heat and simmer until reduced by half. Pour the syrup back over the quince, then cover and refrigerate for 24 hours.

When you're ready to serve the cake, remove the quince halves from the syrup, reserving both. Cut the quinces in half again and remove the seeds.

FOR THE CHOCOLATE SPONGE Preheat the oven to 180°C (350°F). Line three 20 cm (8 inch) round cake tins with baking paper.

Place the eggs and sugar in the bowl of an electric stand mixer and whisk for 7–8 minutes, until thick and pale. Gently fold in the sifted flour with a spoon.

Divide the batter among the three cake tins, spreading to cover the bases. Bake for 7 minutes, checking every few minutes. When ready, the sponge will spring back when gently pressed.

Remove from the oven and leave to cool in the tins.

FOR THE PISTACHIO GANACHE Place the chocolate in a bowl. Pour the cream into a saucepan, bring to boiling point, then pour over the chocolate and mix until smooth. Add the pistachio paste and mix until well combined.

FOR THE PISTACHIO MOUSSE Place the chocolate in a metal bowl over a saucepan of simmering water. Stir until melted and set aside. Using electric beaters, whisk the egg and egg yolks until thick and pale.

Place the sugar and 50 ml (1½ fl oz) water in a saucepan over medium heat. Stir until the sugar has dissolved, then heat until it reaches 121°C (235°F) — the 'soft ball' stage. Squeeze the excess water from the gelatine sheets and add them to the sugar mixture. Stir until the gelatine has dissolved. Slowly pour the hot syrup over the egg mixture, whisking until completely cool.

Add the melted chocolate to the mixture, then the pistachio ganache, mixing to incorporate. Gently fold in the whipped cream.

Dig out a 20 cm (8 inch) round ring, about 6 cm (2½ inches) high; you can use a cake tin with a removable base. Spray or brush with oil and place on a tray.

Place one chocolate sponge inside the ring. Spread a 2 cm (¾ inch) layer of the pistachio mousse over the sponge. Repeat twice, so you have three layers of chocolate sponge and pistachio mousse. Refrigerate for 2–3 hours to set.

TO SERVE Remove the ring and cut the cake into eight pieces. Place on serving plates with the braised quince. Serve drizzled with the quince syrup, garnished with the basil leaves.

This lovely rich tart will keep in the fridge for up to 5 days; bring it to room temperature for serving. To toast the shredded coconut for the crust, and the coconut flakes for the garnish, spread them on separate baking trays and bake in a 170ºC (325ºF) oven for 5–10 minutes, until lightly golden.

Vegan dark chocolate & coconut tart

SERVES 8–12

DATE & COCONUT CRUST

210 g (7½ oz/1¼ cups) medjool dates, pitted

85 g (3 oz/1¼ cups) shredded coconut, toasted

2½ tablespoons ground flaxseeds or ground pepitas (pumpkin seeds)

2½ tablespoons unsweetened cocoa powder

1 tablespoon coconut oil

¼ teaspoon sea salt

DARK CHOCOLATE FILLING

300 g (10½ oz) dark chocolate (70% cocoa), coarsely chopped

400 ml (14 fl oz) coconut milk

80 ml (2½ fl oz/⅓ cup) maple syrup (or liquid sweetener of choice)

1 teaspoon vanilla extract

pinch of sea salt

COCONUT WHIPPED CREAM

400 ml (14 fl oz) coconut milk, chilled overnight

1 tablespoon maple syrup

TO GARNISH

fresh berries, such as strawberries, raspberries, blueberries and blackberries

30 g (1 oz/½ cup) coconut flakes, toasted

FOR THE CRUST Cut two strips of baking paper, each 6 cm (2½ inches) wide, and long enough to hang over the sides of a 23 cm (9 inch) loose-based flan (tart) tin that is about 5 cm (2 inches) deep. Place the paper strips across the tin, to form a cross; these will help you lift the pie out later on. Place a large piece of plastic wrap on top and press it down.

In a food processor, finely chop the dates. When a ball forms, add the remaining ingredients and process until well combined. The dough should stick together when pressed between your fingers; if it doesn't, add a teaspoon of water and process again.

Spoon the mixture into the flan tin. Starting at the centre, press down firmly, moving outwards and up the sides of the tin. Freeze while making the filling.

FOR THE FILLING Place the chocolate in a heatproof bowl over a saucepan of simmering water. When the chocolate is about two-thirds melted, remove from the heat and stir until completely melted and smooth.

Transfer to a large bowl and whisk in the coconut milk until completely smooth. Add the remaining ingredients and whisk again until smooth. Set aside to cool slightly, then spoon into the flan tin, over the crust, smoothing the surface. Chill for 5 hours, or until firm.

FOR THE COCONUT WHIPPED CREAM Scoop the cream from the top of the chilled coconut milk, into a bowl. Add the maple syrup and whip until smooth.

TO SERVE Leave the tart at room temperature for 5–10 minutes. Using the baking paper strips, lift it out of the tin, onto a serving plate. Top with the coconut cream, berries and coconut flakes and serve.

In South-East Asia, where this dessert is really popular, pandan leaves are often used to sweeten desserts and drinks. Once tasted, their delicious flavour is never forgotten. If you can't find leaves, use pandan extract from good Asian grocers. Look for fresh honeycomb in fine food and health food stores.

Beer-battered bananas with fresh honeycomb & pandan ice cream

SERVES 4

FOR THE ICE CREAM Place the milk, cream, pandan leaves, vanilla beans and seeds and half the sugar in a saucepan. Bring to a simmer over medium heat.

In a bowl, mix the egg yolks and remaining sugar. Slowly add the warm milk mixture, stirring constantly.

Pour the mixture into a clean saucepan. Cook, stirring, over medium heat until the temperature reaches 75°C (167°F). Strain the mixture into a clean container and refrigerate for 3–4 hours.

Transfer the mixture to an ice cream maker and churn until just set. Freeze in an airtight container.

FOR THE BEER BATTER Combine the beer and yeast in a small saucepan and warm to body temperature over medium heat. Transfer to a large bowl, whisk in the flours and season with salt and pepper. Cover with a cloth and set aside in a warm place for 30 minutes.

TO COOK THE BANANAS Two-thirds fill a deep-fryer or large heavy-based saucepan with vegetable oil. Heat to 170°C (325°F), or until a cube of bread dropped into the oil turns golden brown in 20 seconds.

Sprinkle the bananas with white rice flour, dusting off any excess. Dip the bananas in the beer batter to lightly coat. Working in two or three batches, slowly lower the bananas into the hot oil, avoiding splashes. Cook for 4–5 minutes, until golden brown. Remove from the oil and drain on paper towel.

TO SERVE Place the warm bananas on a serving plate and season with the salt. Top with the honeycomb, dust with icing sugar and serve with pandan ice cream.

vegetable oil, for deep-frying
3 bananas, peeled and cut into
  quarters
white rice flour, for dusting
1 teaspoon sea salt
3 tablespoons honeycomb, or
  good-quality honey
icing (confectioner's) sugar,
  for dusting

PANDAN ICE CREAM
500 ml (17 fl oz/2 cups) milk
300 ml (10½ fl oz) pouring (single)
  cream
2 pandan leaves
2 vanilla beans, cut in half
  lengthways, seeds scraped
225 g (8 oz/1 cup) caster (superfine)
  sugar
70 g (2½ oz) lightly whisked egg yolks
  (about 3–4 egg yolks)

BEER BATTER
330 ml (11¼ fl oz) lager
1 teaspoon dried yeast
100 g (3½ oz/⅔ cup) plain
  (all-purpose) flour
100 g (3½ oz/⅔ cup) white rice flour

Mini pistachio crème brûlée tarts (page 207)

Vegan dark chocolate & coconut tart (page 202)

Beer-battered bananas with fresh honeycomb & pandan ice cream (page 203)

Brandy snap cigars with strawberry cream (page 206)

Begging for a late-night brandy or Cognac, these cigars make an elegant after-dinner treat. Instead of strawberries, try blueberries or raspberries in the cream.

Brandy snap cigars with strawberry cream

BRANDY SNAPS

90 g (3¼ oz/⅓ cup) unsalted butter

80 g (2¾ oz) brown sugar

50 g (1¾ oz) golden syrup or treacle

80 g (2¾ oz) plain (all-purpose) flour, sifted

1 teaspoon ground ginger

zest of ½ lemon, plus 1 teaspoon lemon juice

1 teaspoon brandy

vegetable oil, for brushing

STRAWBERRY CREAM

250 g (9 oz) strawberries, hulled and halved

100 g (3½ oz) caster (superfine) sugar

1 tablespoon finely grated lemon zest

300 ml (10½ fl oz) thick (double) cream (55% fat)

FOR THE BRANDY SNAPS Preheat the oven to 180°C (350°F). Line two baking trays with baking paper.

Place the butter, sugar and golden syrup in a small saucepan over low heat and heat gently until the butter and sugar have melted.

Place the flour and ginger in a bowl and make a well in the centre. Add the lemon zest, lemon juice and brandy. Pour in the butter mixture and gradually beat until the mixture is smooth.

Dollop teaspoons of the mixture onto the baking trays, spacing them well apart as they will spread. Cook in batches for 8–10 minutes, until set, golden brown and lacy in appearance. Don't let them become too dark as they will taste bitter.

Cool for a minute before making into cigars (see below) — the brandy snaps should still be pliable, but set enough to move without tearing.

FOR THE BRANDY SNAP CIGARS Oil the handle of a wooden spoon and wrap each brandy snap around. If you have a long handle or more than one spoon, you can do a few at a time. Transfer to a rack to cool.

FOR THE STRAWBERRY CREAM Place the strawberries and sugar in a saucepan over medium–low heat. Cook for 5 minutes, or until the strawberries soften and the sugar has dissolved. Cook for a further 5–6 minutes, until the mixture becomes thick and syrupy.

Remove from the heat, stir in the lemon zest and set aside to cool completely.

Whip the cream until firm peaks form, then lightly fold the strawberry mixture through the cream.

TO SERVE Spoon the whipped strawberry cream into a piping (icing) bag and pipe it into the cigars. Serve immediately.

Who doesn't love a brûlée? The pure joy of that sound when you crack the top with a spoon... You'll find lavender compound and pistachio paste in fine food stores. These little tarts are best served the day they are made.

Mini pistachio crème brûlée tarts

MAKES 8

FOR THE CREME BRULEE Heat the milk, cream and half the sugar in a small pan over medium heat, to just below boiling point. Remove from the heat to cool slightly.

In a bowl, combine the egg yolks, egg, pistachio paste and remaining sugar. Slowly add one-third of the milk mixture and mix well, then add the rest and mix until combined. Add the food colouring, to tint the mix a very pale green. Strain into a bowl, cover the surface with plastic wrap, and refrigerate for 2 hours to infuse.

FOR THE LAVENDER CREAM In a small pan, bring the cream and lavender compound to a simmer over low heat; do not boil. Set aside to cool, then strain into a bowl and chill in the fridge for an hour or so. When cold, add the icing sugar and whip to soft peaks.

FOR THE PASTRY Preheat the oven to 175°C (350°F). Set out eight 9 cm (3½ inch) tart (flan) tins, about 2 cm (¾ inch) deep. Roll the puff pastry out 5 mm (¼ inch) thick, then pierce all over with a fork. Cut the pastry slightly larger than the tins, then line the tins and trim the pastry edges. Chill in the fridge for 20 minutes.

Line the pastry cases with baking paper and fill with dried rice, beans or baking beads. Bake for 14 minutes, remove the baking paper and beads, then bake for another 5–10 minutes, until the pastry is golden brown. Remove from the oven and leave to cool slightly. Turn the oven down to 95°C (200°F).

Pour the crème brûlée mix into the tart shells, filling to the top. Bake for 20–30 minutes, or until the custard has just set. Leave to cool completely.

TO SERVE Sprinkle the sugar over the tarts. Carefully use a kitchen blow torch to caramelise the sugar, or place under a hot grill (broiler). Serve with the lavender cream.

225 g (8 oz) puff pastry
100 g (3½ oz) caster (superfine) sugar

PISTACHIO CREME BRULEE
125 ml (4 fl oz/½ cup) milk
375 ml (13 fl oz/1½ cups) pouring (single) cream
85 g (3 oz) caster (superfine) sugar
5 free-range egg yolks
½ lightly beaten free-range egg
45 g (1¾ oz) pistachio paste
1 drop green food colouring

LAVENDER CREAM
300 ml (10½ fl oz) pouring (single) cream
1½ teaspoons lavender compound
60 g (2¼ oz/½ cup) icing (confectioners') sugar, sifted

I managed to get my hands on this recipe from my good mate Mario Batali. We were in New York on the night of a massive blizzard and most of the restaurants were closed, so he invited me to his home for dinner, where he cooked about ten different desserts for us — this one being my favourite of them all. So of course I asked him for the recipe, so I could let you try it too.

My friend Mario's baked maple cheesecakes

MAKES 6

RASPBERRY PUREE
150 g (5½ oz) frozen raspberries
40 g (1½ oz) caster (superfine) sugar
2 teaspoons lemon juice
⅓ teaspoon finely grated lemon zest

CHEESECAKES
unsalted butter, for greasing
50 g (1¾ oz) raw caster (superfine) sugar,
    for coating the moulds
225 g (8 oz) pure maple syrup
70 ml (2¼ oz) pouring (single) cream
115 g (4 oz) cream cheese, at room
    temperature
25 g (1 oz) caster (superfine) sugar
1½ large lightly beaten free-range eggs
½ teaspoon vanilla bean seeds (scraped
    from a vanilla pod)
225 g (8 oz) mascarpone cheese

TO GARNISH
fresh raspberries

FOR THE RASPBERRY PUREE Place all the ingredients in a small saucepan over medium heat and bring to a simmer. Remove from the heat to cool for 10 minutes.

Place in a food processor and blend until smooth. Strain through a fine sieve, pressing down with a spoon to push the fruit and juices through. Discard the raspberry seeds.

Transfer the purée to an airtight container and refrigerate until ready to serve. The purée will keep for several days.

FOR THE CHEESECAKES Butter six 125 ml (4 fl oz/½ cup) metal dariole moulds. Sprinkle them with the raw caster sugar, evenly coating the bottom and sides. Tap out the excess sugar and place the moulds in a roasting tin.

Bring the maple syrup to the boil in large, heavy-based saucepan over medium–high heat. Reduce the heat to medium and boil gently for 30 minutes, stirring occasionally, until the maple syrup has reduced by one-third; the syrup will bubble vigorously.

Remove from the heat and carefully stir in the cream — the mixture will bubble up! Return the saucepan to the heat and simmer until any crystallised pieces have dissolved. Remove from the heat and leave to cool completely.

Preheat the oven to 160°C (315°F).

Using an electric mixer, beat the cream cheese and caster sugar in a large bowl until smooth. Add the eggs and vanilla seeds and beat for 1 minute, then add the mascarpone cheese and beat until just blended and smooth.

Add a small amount of the cheese mixture to the pot of maple syrup mix and mix together. Running the mixer on low speed, pour the syrup mixture into the mixing bowl and mix until combined and smooth.

Divide the batter among the moulds. Add enough hot water to the roasting tin to come halfway up the sides of the moulds.

Transfer to the roasting tin to the oven and bake for about 1 hour, until the cheesecakes are light golden on top, and the centres move slightly when gently shaken.

Remove the roasting tin from the oven. Leave the moulds to cool in the water bath for 15 minutes. Remove the moulds from the water and refrigerate uncovered overnight.

The cheesecakes can be prepared 2 days in advance, so if leaving them longer, cover with plastic wrap and keep refrigerated.

TO SERVE Remove the cheesecakes from the fridge. Run a small sharp knife around the side of the moulds to loosen them.

Invert the cheesecakes onto serving plates, shaking gently to release them. Garnish each cheesecake with fresh raspberries and a drizzle of raspberry purée.

Calvados is an apple liqueur that you will find in good liquor stores.
You can use a good dessert wine or sticky in place of the sauternes.

Calvados custards with brown butter crumble & sauternes apple

MAKES 8

CALVADOS CUSTARDS
165 ml (5½ fl oz/⅔ cup) milk
165 ml (5½ fl oz/⅔ cup) pouring
(single) cream
½ vanilla bean, cut in half
lengthways, seeds scraped
75 g (2½ oz) caster (superfine) sugar
2 free-range eggs yolks
30 ml (1 fl oz) Calvados

BROWN BUTTER CRUMBLE
125 g (4½ oz) unsalted butter
125 g (4½ oz) skim milk powder

SAUTERNES APPLE
100 ml (3½ fl oz) sauternes or
moscato wine
1 tablespoon lemon juice
1 kg (2 lb 4 oz) granny smith apples
100 g (3½ oz) unsalted butter
80 g (2¾ oz) caster (superfine) sugar
1 teaspoon ground cinnamon
¼ teaspoon ground cardamom

TO SERVE
155 g (5½ oz/¾ cup) raw (demerara)
sugar
8 scoops good-quality vanilla
ice cream

FOR THE CUSTARDS Combine the milk, cream, vanilla seeds and half the sugar in a saucepan. Bring to just below boiling, then set aside to cool slightly.

In a bowl, mix the egg yolks and remaining sugar. Whisk in the warm cream mixture until combined, strain into a container, then mix in the Calvados. Cover the surface with plastic wrap and chill for at least 8 hours.

The next day, preheat the oven to 95°C (190°F). Give the custard a good stir, then pour into eight small 10 cm (3 inch) baking dishes. Bake for 30 minutes, or until the custards are fully set, but still with a little wobble. Cool to room temperature.

FOR THE BROWN BUTTER CRUMBLE Melt the butter in a saucepan over medium heat. Add the milk powder and whisk constantly until the butter and milk powder turn golden brown. Strain the crumble mixture over a bowl, keeping the strained butter, and placing the crumble on a tray lined with baking paper to cool.

FOR THE APPLE In a bowl, combine the sauternes and lemon juice. Peel and core the apples, then cut each into about six wedges. Toss in the sauternes mixture.

In a large frying pan over medium–high heat, melt half the butter. Add half the apple, sugar and spices and cook for 1 minute. Add half the sauternes mixture and cook for 3–4 minutes. Reduce the heat and cook until the apple is soft and no juice remains. Remove the apple and cook the remaining wedges the same way.

TO SERVE Sprinkle the sugar evenly over the custards and carefully caramelise with a kitchen blowtorch, or place under a hot grill (broiler). Top with the apple wedges, crumble mix and a dollop of ice cream.

In the Maldives, sweets and desserts are an important part of the meal, and are traditionally based around coconut and fruits such as mangoes and bananas. This is my version of a traditional Maldivian custard, which I served as part of a dinner event there. We included persimmons, cinnamon, ginger and some nuts and herbs to give it a really fresh, vibrant look and taste.

Maldivian baked custard with persimmon & pomegranate

½ pomegranate, cut into 6 wedges, seeds reserved
80 g (2¾ oz) macadamia nuts, toasted, very roughly chopped
12 Vietnamese mint leaves

MALDIVIAN CUSTARD
2 teaspoons cardamom seeds
2 pandan leaves
100 g (3½ oz) caster (superfine) sugar
250 ml (9 fl oz/1 cup) coconut milk
35 g (1¼ oz) cornflour (cornstarch)

POACHED PERSIMMONS
6 firm, ripe persimmons
125 ml (4 fl oz/½ cup) dry white wine
185 ml (6 fl oz/¾ cup) strained fresh orange juice
55 g (2 oz/¼ cup) caster (superfine) sugar
1 teaspoon grated fresh ginger
¼ teaspoon ground cinnamon

FOR THE CUSTARD Place the cardamom, pandan leaves and sugar in a saucepan. Pour in 500 ml (17 fl oz/2 cups) water and bring to the boil over medium heat. Remove from the heat and strain into a bowl.

Whisk the coconut milk and cornflour together in a bowl, then add the pandan water and whisk until combined.

Transfer the mixture to a clean saucepan and whisk over medium heat until it comes to the boil. Pour into a 22 cm (8½ inch) round shallow serving dish and place in the fridge 2–3 hours, or until cold and set.

FOR THE PERSIMMONS Bring a large saucepan of water to the boil. Carefully drop the whole persimmons into the water. Cook for about 15–20 seconds, then remove and refresh in iced water. Peel the persimmons and cut each into eight wedges, discarding any seeds.

Place the persimmon wedges in a clean saucepan. Add the remaining ingredients and bring to the boil, stirring occasionally. Reduce the heat and simmer, covered, for 10 minutes, or until the persimmon is tender. Remove the persimmon wedges with a slotted spoon, place in a bowl, and set aside to cool.

Bring the persimmon syrup back to the boil and continue to cook until reduced to about 125 ml (4 fl oz/½ cup). Pour the syrup over the persimmons, then refrigerate for 2 hours.

TO SERVE Arrange the persimmon and pomegranate seeds over the top of the custard. Garnish with the macadamias and mint leaves.

These little bars are really quite decadent, and perfect for sharing as an after-dinner sweet when a full dessert is too much. As always, using quality chocolate will make all the difference.

Bounty bars

Line a baking tray with baking paper.

Place the butter and sugar in an electric mixer bowl and beat on medium speed until pale and creamy. Reduce the speed to low and gradually add the condensed milk, beating constantly, until smooth. Add the coconut and beat on medium speed until combined.

Divide the mixture into 15 portions and shape into rectangles. Place on the baking tray and freeze for 3 hours.

Place two-thirds of the chopped chocolate in a microwave-safe bowl. Microwave on medium power for 30 seconds, stir, then repeat at 15-second intervals until the chocolate has melted. Add the remaining chocolate and stir until it has melted. (This is called tempering, and gives the chocolate a glossy texture and sets it correctly.)

Remove the bars from the freezer. Using two forks, dip a bar into the melted chocolate and roll to coat all sides. Use one fork to remove the bar from the chocolate and the other to wipe off the excess chocolate. Place the bar back on the lined baking tray. Repeat with the remaining bars, then sprinkle the bars with the smoked sea salt.

Refrigerate for 1 hour, to set the chocolate. Bring to room temperature for 30 minutes before serving.

The bars will keep in an airtight container in the fridge for up to 1 week.

75 g (2½ oz) unsalted butter, softened
65 g (2¼ oz) caster (superfine) sugar
395 g (14 oz/1¼ cups) sweetened condensed milk
300 g (10½ oz/3⅓ cups) desiccated (shredded) coconut
250 g (9 oz) dark chocolate, chopped
1 teaspoon smoked sea salt or pink sea salt

The peanut brittle can be made up to a week in advance. You can double the quantity and serve the extra brittle on its own, or over some good vanilla ice cream. You can also do the same with the caramel sauce.

Banana parfait with peanut brittle & salted caramel sauce

SERVES 6

BANANA PARFAIT
50 g (1¾ oz) brown sugar
2 teaspoons dark rum
2 teaspoons lime juice
1 star anise
1 cinnamon stick
2 small overripe bananas, peeled and
    roughly chopped
525 ml (18 fl oz) pouring (single) cream
1 gelatine sheet (gold strength), softened in
    cold water for 5 minutes
1 teaspoon sea salt
170 g (6 oz) caster (superfine) sugar
5 free-range egg yolks
1 tablespoon roasted peanuts, roughly
    chopped

PEANUT BRITTLE
½ teaspoon bicarbonate of soda
    (baking soda)
110 g (3¾ oz/½ cup) caster (superfine) sugar
80 ml (2½ fl oz/⅓ cup) liquid glucose
1 tablespoon unsalted butter
150 g (5½ oz) raw peanuts

SALTED CARAMEL SAUCE
80 g (2¾ oz) caster (superfine) sugar
35 g (1¼ oz) cold unsalted butter,
    roughly chopped
pinch of sea salt
125 ml (4 fl oz/½ cup) pouring (single)
    cream, warmed

FOR THE BANANA PARFAIT Place the brown sugar in a small saucepan with the rum, lime juice, star anise and cinnamon stick. Stir over medium heat until the sugar has dissolved. Add the banana and cook for 3–5 minutes, or until softened. Discard the cinnamon and star anise.

Add 150 ml (5 fl oz) of the cream, stirring to combine and warm through. Squeeze the excess water from the gelatine sheets and add them to the banana mixture with the salt. Stir until the gelatine has dissolved, then transfer the mixture to a blender and blend until smooth. Set aside.

Line an 11 x 26 cm (4¼ x 10½ inch) loaf (bar) tin with baking paper.

Place the caster sugar and 60 ml (2 fl oz/ ¼ cup) water in a small saucepan over medium heat, stirring until the sugar has dissolved. Bring to the boil and cook for 4–6 minutes, until the mixture reaches 120°C (235°F) on a sugar thermometer.

Meanwhile, whisk the egg yolks using an electric mixer for 3–4 minutes, until pale and fluffy. Gradually add the hot sugar syrup and whisk on medium speed for 4–5 minutes, until cooled to room temperature.

Whip the remaining 375 ml (13 fl oz/1½ cups) cream to soft peaks.

Using a large spoon, gently fold the banana mixture into the egg yolk mixture, then the whipped cream and roasted peanuts. Pour into lined loaf tin and smooth the surface. Refrigerate overnight to set.

FOR THE PEANUT BRITTLE Line a baking tray with a silicon mat or baking paper. Combine the bicarbonate of soda and ¾ teaspoon water in a small bowl.

Place the sugar, glucose and 125 ml (4 fl oz/ ½ cup) water in a saucepan. Bring to the boil and cook until the temperature reaches 115°C (230°F) on a sugar thermometer. Add the butter and peanuts and continue to cook, stirring, until golden in colour and a temperature of 148°C (300°F) is reached. Remove from the heat.

Add the bicarbonate of soda mixture and stir until the mixture starts to foam, then pour onto prepared baking tray. Working quickly, use a rolling pin or spatula to spread the mixture thinly. Set aside to cool.

FOR THE CARAMEL SAUCE Place the sugar and 50 ml (1½ fl oz) water in a small saucepan over low heat and stir until the sugar has dissolved. Increase the heat to high and cook for 4–5 minutes, until a dark caramel colour.

Carefully whisk in the butter, a little at a time, taking care as the caramel may spit. Add the salt, then slowly whisk in the warm cream.

Reduce the heat to low and simmer gently for 5 minutes, until slightly thickened. Cool and refrigerate until required.

TO SERVE Cut the parfait into six pieces and place on a large serving plate. Drizzle with the caramel sauce. Break the peanut brittle into shards and sprinkle over the top.

Pineapple and coconut go so well together. This is a beautifully refreshing dessert on a hot day, or after a heavy, spicy meal.

Coconut panna cotta with marinated pineapple, pink peppercorns & fennel

MAKES 8

FOR THE MARINATED PINEAPPLE Preheat the oven to 160°C (315°F).

Mix together the rum, sugar syrup, vanilla seeds and pod to make a syrup. Place the pineapple in a baking dish and pour the syrup over the top. Add the cinnamon sticks.

Cover with foil and bake for 1½ hours. Cool for 30 minutes, then refrigerate in the syrup for 24 hours.

Just before serving, slice the pineapple very thinly, keeping the syrup.

FOR THE PANNA COTTA Place the palm sugar and coconut water in a small saucepan over low heat. Stir until the sugar has melted, making sure the coconut water does not boil.

Squeeze the excess water from the gelatine sheets. Add them to the saucepan and stir until dissolved.

Place a large bowl over ice. Strain the mixture into the bowl and add the coconut milk and cream. Stir until the mixture has cooled.

Lightly oil eight 125 ml (4 fl oz/½ cup) ramekins or dariole moulds. Pour the mixture into them and refrigerate for 4 hours, or until set.

TO SERVE Turn the panna cottas out onto serving plates. Arrange the pineapple slices around and drizzle with a little pineapple syrup. Garnish with the young coconut flesh, fennel fronds and pink peppercorns.

1 young coconut, flesh roughly torn, juice reserved for the panna cotta
fennel fronds
2 teaspoons pink peppercorns, lightly toasted and lightly crushed

MARINATED PINEAPPLE
100 ml (3½ fl oz) Malibu or other coconut rum
300 ml (10½ fl oz) plain Sugar syrup (page 232)
1 vanilla bean, cut in half lengthways, seeds scraped
1 pineapple, peeled, cored and quartered lengthways
2 cinnamon sticks, broken into pieces

COCONUT PANNA COTTA
75 g (2¾ oz) palm sugar (jaggery), roughly chopped
250 ml (9 fl oz/1 cup) coconut water (from the fresh coconut)
2¾ gelatine sheets (gold strength), soaked in cold water for 5 minutes
95 ml (3¼ fl oz) coconut milk
95 ml (3¼ fl oz) coconut cream
oil, for greasing

If you're pushed for time, buy a good-quality cherry sorbet for this dessert instead of making it from scratch. The peanut butter parfait can be made up to a week in advance and kept in the freezer.

Peanut butter ice-cream sandwiches with dulce de leche, strawberry jus & cherry sorbet

MAKES 8 SANDWICHES

CHERRY SORBET
900 g (2 lb) cherries, stems and
    stones removed
65 g (2¼ oz) caster (superfine) sugar
juice of ½ lemon

DULCE DE LECHE
395 g (13¾ oz) tin of sweetened
    condensed milk

STRAWBERRY JUS
300 g (10½ oz) frozen strawberries
30 g (1 oz) caster (superfine) sugar
1 vanilla bean, cut in half lengthways,
    seeds scraped
500 g (1 lb 2 oz) strawberries, hulled

PEANUT BUTTER PARFAIT
1½ free-range egg yolks
35 g (1¼ oz) caster (superfine) sugar
100 ml (3½ fl oz) milk
½ vanilla bean, cut in half lengthways,
    seeds scraped
1¾ gelatine sheets (gold strength),
    soaked in cold water for 5 minutes
40 g (1½ oz) peanut butter
2 teaspoons liquid glucose
1 free-range egg white
150 ml (5 fl oz) pouring (single) cream
25 g (1 oz) salted peanuts, chopped

CHOCOLATE SABLE DOUGH
250 g (9 oz) unsalted butter, softened
140 g (5 oz) icing (confectioners') sugar
3 free-range egg yolks
300 g (10½ oz/2 cups) plain (all-purpose)
    flour, plus extra for kneading
75 g (2½ oz/⅔ cup) unsweetened
    cocoa powder

FOR THE CHERRY SORBET Place the cherries in a saucepan with the sugar and 250 ml (9 fl oz/1 cup) water. Cook over medium heat for 10–15 minutes, until the cherries are very soft. Set aside to cool to room temperature. Refrigerate until thoroughly chilled.

Purée the mixture in a blender, then strain, discarding the pulp. Add the lemon juice.

Pour into an ice cream machine and churn until just set. Transfer to an airtight container and keep in the freezer until needed.

FOR THE DULCE DE LECHE Remove the label from the unopened tin of condensed milk. Fill a deep, medium-sized saucepan with water and bring to the boil. Carefully place the tin in the saucepan, ensuring there is enough water to completely cover the tin at all times. Simmer, uncovered, for 3 hours, topping up the water frequently during this time. Carefully remove the tin from the boiling water. Allow to cool completely before opening.

FOR THE STRAWBERRY JUS Combine the strawberries, sugar and the vanilla seeds and pod in a heatproof bowl. Wrap the bowl tightly with plastic wrap and set it over a saucepan of simmering water for 2 hours. Check the water regularly to ensure it doesn't boil dry.

Strain into a bowl and, while still warm, add the fresh strawberries. Allow to cool down at room temperature for a few hours, so the strawberries absorb the juice.

FOR THE PARFAIT Dig out an 11 x 26 cm (4¼ x 10½ inch) tray, with sides at least 2 cm (¾ inch) deep. Line with baking paper.

Combine the egg yolks and half the sugar in a bowl and whisk until pale and fluffy.

Combine the milk and vanilla seeds in a small saucepan and bring to just below boiling point, then pour the hot milk into the egg mixture, whisking to combine.

Squeeze out the excess water from the gelatine leaves, then add them to the milk mixture and stir until dissolved.

Place the peanut butter in a bowl. Strain the milk mixture over and mix until smooth.

In another saucepan, combine the remaining sugar with the glucose and 2 teaspoons water. Place over medium heat and bring to 121°C (235°F). Immediately pour into an electric mixer bowl with the egg white and whisk until medium peaks form. Fold into the peanut mixture.

Whip the cream to soft peaks and fold into the peanut mixture with the chopped peanuts. Pour the mixture onto the prepared tray. Freeze for at least 2 hours.

FOR THE CHOCOLATE SABLE DOUGH Place the butter and icing sugar in a bowl and mix until combined.

Add the egg yolks, flour and cocoa powder and mix until just combined, taking care not to over-mix. Turn out onto a lightly floured surface and knead the dough until almost smooth. Shape into a disc and cover with plastic wrap. Refrigerate for 1 hour.

Leave the dough at room temperature for 10–15 minutes. Meanwhile, preheat the oven to 160°C (315°F).

On a sheet of baking paper, roll the dough out to a 3 mm (⅛ inch) thickness. Cut 12 rectangles measuring 4 x 11 cm (1½ x 4¼ inches). Place on a baking tray lined with fresh baking paper and bake for 12–15 minutes, until firm. Remove from the oven and leave to cool.

TO ASSEMBLE Place a chocolate sable on each serving plate. Cut the frozen peanut butter parfait into six pieces and place on each sable. Pour over the dulce de leche. Top with another sable to form a sandwich.

Serve the strawberry jus and cherry sorbet on the side.

Peanut butter ice-cream sandwiches with dulce de leche, strawberry jus & cherry sorbet (page 218)

Soft Swiss meringue with berries
& almond anglaise (page 222)

Instead of slicing the meringue, you can serve this marvellous dinner party dessert in the middle of the table for guests to help themselves to, with the raspberry coulis and almond anglaise in separate jugs for a theatrical drizzle.

Soft Swiss meringue with berries & almond anglaise

RASPBERRY COULIS
65 ml (2 fl oz) plain Sugar syrup (page 232)
300 g (10½ fl oz) raspberry purée (you can use store-bought, or the one from Mario's cheesecake on page 208)

MERINGUE
4 free-range egg whites
220 g (7¾ oz/1 cup) caster (superfine) sugar, plus extra for dusting

RASPBERRY FILLING
400 ml (14 fl oz) thick (double) cream
100 g (3½ oz) raspberries, crushed

ALMOND ANGLAISE
250 ml (9 fl oz/1 cup) milk
250 ml (9 fl oz/1 cup) pouring (single) cream
75 g (2½ oz/⅓ cup) caster (superfine) sugar
4 free-range egg yolks
Frangelico or almond liqueur, to taste

TO GARNISH
150 g (5½ oz) strawberries, halved
150 g (5½ oz) blackberries
150 g (5½ oz) raspberries
70 g (2½ oz) flaked almonds, toasted
icing (confectioners') sugar, for dusting

FOR THE RASPBERRY COULIS Place the sugar syrup and raspberry purée in a saucepan over medium heat and bring to a simmer. Remove from the heat and cool in the fridge.

FOR THE MERINGUE Preheat the oven to 180°C (350°F). Line a 23 x 33 cm (9 x 13 inch) Swiss roll (jelly roll) tin with baking paper.

Place the egg whites in a clean mixer bowl and whisk with electric beaters until medium peaks form. Gradually add the sugar, a tablespoon at a time, whisking until very stiff and glossy.

Spoon the mixture into the lined roll tin and smooth the surface. Bake for 8 minutes, or until golden brown.

Reduce the oven temperature to 160°C (315°F) and bake for a further 15 minutes, or until the meringue is crispy.

Sprinkle a sheet of baking paper with extra caster sugar. Turn the meringue out onto the baking paper, and peel off the baking paper from the base of the meringue. Leave to cool.

FOR THE RASPBERRY FILLING Place the cream and raspberries in a bowl and lightly mix together.

FOR THE ALMOND ANGLAISE Place the milk, cream and half the sugar in a saucepan and bring to boiling point.

In a metal bowl, mix the egg yolks and remaining sugar. Whisk in half the milk mixture, then add the remaining liquid and whisk until well combined.

Pour into a clean saucepan and heat gently, stirring constantly until the mixture reaches 84°C (183°F) and coats the back of a spoon, taking care not to overcook the custard or the egg will scramble. Set aside to cool, then add the almond liqueur to taste.

TO SERVE Spread the raspberry filling evenly over the meringue. Top with three-quarters of the strawberries, blackberries and raspberries. Starting at the long end, roll up the meringue, using the baking paper to help you.

Cut into slices and place in serving bowls. Drizzle with the raspberry coulis. Top with the remaining fresh berries and scatter the flaked almonds over. Dust with icing sugar and serve the almond anglaise alongside.

Chapter 9

Basics

A good collection of basic pantry recipes is a fabulous tool for creating really exciting dishes at home. Good sauces and dressings can form the basis of a great meal, and can also transform a simple dish into something just that little bit fancy.

A few of the recipes in this chapter feature more than once in the book — the knockout garlic aioli on page 228 works well with both the tempura mussel po boys (page 122) and patatas bravas (page 77), and the beautiful wasabi dressing on page 233 is great drizzled over tempura oysters (page 84) and raw tuna pizzettas (page 92). And then there's Mum's wickedly good tomato relish on page 233 — that, if you ask me, can go on just about anything.

Beautifully, many of these recipes also keep well in the fridge, so they can be made in advance and pulled out just as you need them, streamlining preparation on the day.

Use these basic recipes as a guide and don't be afraid to adjust the spices or heat to your own taste.

Kimchi is a traditional Korean side dish made of vegetables and chillies. Koreans eat it at nearly every meal, and it can be used fresh or fermented. It gives the mini hot dogs on page 158 a good punch of flavour and is so easy to prepare.

Cabbage kimchi

MAKES 1 CABBAGE

Cut the cabbage in half. Wash in cold water, then drain well. Rub the salt into the leaves and place the cabbage halves in a bowl. Cover with plastic wrap and set aside for 4 hours at room temperature.

Rinse the cabbage halves under cold running water, squeezing as much water out of the leaves as possible.

Place the sugar and tapioca flour in a small saucepan. Stir in 185 ml (6 fl oz/¾ cup) water and bring to a simmer over medium heat. Cook for 3–4 minutes, until the mixture has thickened. Remove from the heat and leave to cool.

In a small bowl, whisk together the fish sauce and chilli powder. Add to the tapioca mixture and mix until well combined. Stir in the garlic, onion, ginger and oysters until well combined.

Put the cabbage halves in a large bowl. Wearing kitchen gloves, gently push the spring onion and leek in between the cabbage leaves. Rub the tapioca mixture through the cabbage, ensuring it goes in between the leaves.

Wrap the bowl well with plastic wrap, so that no air can escape at all. Leave in a cool place for 3 days. Your cabbage is then ready to be eaten.

Freeze the kimchi if you are not going to use it all within a week.

1 Chinese cabbage
100 g (3½ oz) fine sea salt
55 g (2 oz/¼ cup) caster (superfine) sugar
25 g (1 oz) tapioca flour
3 tablespoons fish sauce
50 g (1¾ oz) chilli powder
40 g (1½ oz) garlic cloves, finely chopped
½ onion, finely chopped
4 cm (1½ inch) piece of fresh ginger, peeled and finely chopped
10 oysters, roughly chopped
6 spring onions (scallions), roughly chopped
½ large leek, white part only, thinly sliced

You'll find good-quality cabernet sauvignon vinegar in speciality grocers. Look for Spanish ones aged in oak barrels.

Cabernet sauvignon dressing

MAKES 300 ML (10½ FL OZ)

75 ml (2¼ fl oz) good-quality cabernet
   sauvignon vinegar
225 ml (7¾ fl oz) extra virgin olive oil

Place the vinegar and olive oil in a sterile jar with a lid. Seal the lid on and shake well.

Keep in the refrigerator and use as required; it will keep for 2–3 months in the fridge. Bring to room temperature for serving.

Tinned chipotle chillies are stocked in delis and spice shops. If you'd like a bit of heat in your mayo, add a little more chipotle purée.

Chipotle mayonnaise

MAKES ABOUT 350 G (12 OZ/1½ CUPS)

60 g (2¼ oz) chipotle chillies in adobo sauce
250 g (9 oz) mayonnaise
1½ tablespoons lime juice

Blend the chipotle chillies in a small food processor to form a paste. Push through a sieve, into a bowl.

Add the mayonnaise and the lime juice and stir to combine.

Store in an airtight container in the fridge, where it will keep for up to 2 weeks.

Adding a sprinkling of these is a great way to dress simple steamed green beans, or to add extra flavour and texture to Asian salads.

Crisp shallots & garlic

MAKES ABOUT 2 CUPS

500 ml (17 fl oz/2 cups) vegetable oil
500 g (1 lb 2 oz) red Asian shallots or French shallots, thinly sliced
300 g (10½ oz) garlic cloves, thinly sliced

Heat the vegetable oil in a wok or saucepan over medium heat to 170°C (325°F), or until a cube of bread dropped into the oil turns golden brown in 20 seconds.

Add half the shallot and garlic and slowly cook for 6–8 minutes, or until golden brown, stirring occasionally. Remove with a slotted spoon and drain on paper towels. Repeat with the remaining shallot and garlic.

Once fully cooled, transfer to an airtight container; they will keep in a cool place for up to 4 weeks.

A dressing such as this can turn the simplest salad or dish into something marvellous. This dressing can be refrigerated in an airtight container for up to 3 months. The longer you leave it, the more the flavours will develop.

Curry dressing

MAKES ABOUT 200 ML (7 FL OZ)

2 teaspoons curry powder
200 ml (7 fl oz) olive oil
2½ tablespoons cabernet sauvignon vinegar

Lightly toast the curry powder in a small frying pan over medium heat for 2 minutes, or until fragrant. Add the olive oil, reduce the heat to low, and gently heat the oil through. When warm, remove from the heat and leave to cool.

Pour the curry oil into a clean airtight container and set aside for 24 hours.

Pass the curry oil through a fine filter or coffee filter paper, into a sterile jar with a lid. Add the vinegar, screw the lid on and shake well.

Keep in the fridge and use as required.

Serve this beautiful potato mash as a side to any meat or seafood dish. If you have trouble sourcing fontina cheese from good delicatessens and cheese shops, use a good-quality gouda.

Fontina mash

315 g (11 oz/1 cup) rock salt
4 large desiree or other mashing potatoes
80 ml (2½ fl oz/⅓ cup) milk
100 ml (3½ fl oz) single (pouring) cream
50 g (1¾ oz) unsalted butter
100 g (3½ oz) fontina, grated
70 g (2½ oz) parmesan, grated
extra virgin olive oil, for drizzling

Preheat the oven to 180°C (350°F).

Place a thin layer of rock salt on a baking tray, then place the potatoes on top. Bake for 1½ hours, until a knife goes straight through them. While still hot, scoop out the flesh and pass it through a mouli, or mash well.

Place the potatoes, milk, cream and butter in a saucepan over low heat. Use a spatula or wooden spoon to mash combine. Add the cheeses and heat for a few minutes until the cheese has melted. Season with salt and pepper.

Scoop the mash into a bowl and drizzle with extra virgin olive oil. Serve warm.

This aioli really packs a punch and is great on just about anything, from a roast chicken sandwich to a dipping sauce for crispy fried calamari.

Garlic aioli

MAKES ABOUT 500 G (2 CUPS)

150 g (5½ oz) Garlic confit (page 229), passed through a fine sieve
350 g (12 oz) mayonnaise
juice of 1 lemon

Combine all the ingredients in a bowl, whisking to combine.

Place in an airtight container and use as required. The aioli will keep for up to 1 week in the refrigerator.

'Confit' means to slowly cook, which is the perfect way to take the rawness and pungency from garlic. Stir your garlic confit through mash potato or mayonnaise for extra kick.

Garlic confit

MAKES ABOUT 200 G (7 OZ)

200 g (7 oz) garlic cloves
600 ml (21 fl oz) milk
300 ml (10½ fl oz) extra virgin olive oil

Peel the garlic cloves and place in a saucepan. Cover with 200 ml (7 fl oz) of the milk. Bring to the boil, then strain.

Place the garlic back in the pan and cover with another 200 ml (7 fl oz) of the milk. Bring to the boil, then strain.

Repeat the process a third time, using the remaining milk.

Drain, then rinse the garlic in cold water. Place the garlic in a clean saucepan and cover with the olive oil. Cook the garlic very slowly for 30 minutes, or until tender.

Remove the garlic cloves with a slotted spoon, reserving the oil. Place the garlic in a blender. Begin blending, adding a little of the reserved garlic oil to form a paste. Season with salt and pepper.

Transfer to a sterilised jar and use as required. The confit will keep in the refrigerator for up to 10 days.

Made to my mum's recipe, this chutney is always in my fridge. It's perfect on steak sandwiches and alongside simple fish dishes.

Green tomato chutney

MAKES ABOUT 250 G (9 OZ)

½ teaspoon green cardamom pods
⅛ teaspoon ground turmeric
½ cinnamon stick
1 small garlic clove, finely chopped
1.5 cm (⅝ inch) piece of fresh ginger, peeled and finely chopped
½ onion, finely chopped
500 g (1 lb 2 oz) green tomatoes, cores removed, finely chopped
½ green apple, peeled, cored and chopped
100 g (3½ oz/½ cup) soft brown sugar
45 g (1½ oz/¼ cup) raisins
100 ml (3½ fl oz) cider vinegar

Crush the cardamom seeds, discarding the pods. Add the cardamom seeds to a large saucepan and toast for 30 seconds over medium heat.

Stir in the remaining ingredients and cook for 45 minutes, or until the chutney is nice and thick. Season with salt and pepper.

Remove from the heat and spread the chutney on a flat tray, then place in the refrigerator to chill quickly.

Once chilled, spoon into sterilised jars and use as required. The chutney will keep in the refrigerator for 3–4 weeks.

Yuzu is an aromatic Japanese citrus fruit. Fresh is best but can be hard to obtain, however bottled yuzu juice is sold in some Japanese specialty grocers and fine food stores. Instead of making your own mayonnaise in this recipe, you can simply mix the yuzu juice, wasabi and miso paste through 400 g (14 oz) of a good-quality mayo.

Miso mayo

MAKES ABOUT 2 CUPS

1 tablespoon dijon mustard
2 large free-range egg yolks
2 tablespoons white wine vinegar
45 ml (1½ fl oz) yuzu juice or lime juice, to taste
300 ml (10½ fl oz) vegetable oil
2 tablespoons grated fresh wasabi (or good-quality frozen wasabi)
70 g (2½ oz) white miso paste

Place the mustard, egg yolks, vinegar and yuzu juice in a bowl. Begin whisking while slowly adding the vegetable oil.

Whisk in the wasabi and miso until well combined.

Store the mayo in a clean airtight container in the fridge; it will keep for up to 2 weeks.

Here is a lovely way to caramelise onions, to bring out their natural sugars. Onion confit is great on burgers!

Onion confit

MAKES ABOUT 1 CUP

100 g (3½ oz) butter
2 large onions, thinly sliced
100 ml (3½ fl oz) honey
100 ml (3½ fl oz) white wine
50 ml (1¾ fl oz) sherry vinegar or balsamic vinegar

Melt the butter in a heavy-based saucepan. Add the onion and cook over low heat for 10 minutes, stirring occasionally.

Stir in the honey and wine and cook over very low heat for 45–50 minutes, or until the mixture has a jam-like consistency.

Stir the vinegar through and season to taste with salt and pepper.

Transfer to a sterilised jar and use as required. The confit will keep in the refrigerator for up to 2 weeks.

Romesco is a Spanish red sauce often served with fish dishes; it is also wonderful with chicken and vegetables. For a spicier romesco, add a little more dried ancho chilli.

Romesco sauce

MAKES ABOUT 2 CUPS

500 g (1 lb 2 oz) tinned tomatoes
170 ml (5½ fl oz/⅔ cup) extra virgin olive oil
1 dried ancho chilli
140 g (5 oz) hazelnuts, toasted, skins rubbed off with a tea towel while warm
50 g (1¾ oz) blanched almonds
2 slices firm white bread, cut into 1 cm (½ inch) cubes
4 large garlic cloves, sliced
¼ teaspoon chilli flakes
1 red capsicum (pepper), roasted and peeled
2 tablespoons cabernet sauvignon vinegar

Preheat the oven to 200°C (400°F). Line a baking tray with foil, add the tomatoes to the tray and roast in the oven for 10 minutes.

Heat the olive oil in a frying pan over medium heat. Add the dried ancho chilli and cook for 20–30 seconds, stirring, until fragrant and a brighter red colour. Remove the chilli to a bowl, using a slotted spoon.

Add the hazelnuts, almonds, bread, garlic and chilli flakes to the oil and cook, stirring, for 2–3 minutes, until the bread and garlic are golden. Add the mixture, including the oil, to the chilli in the bowl and cool slightly.

Transfer the mixture to a food processor. Add the capsicum, vinegar and roasted tomatoes. Process until smooth, then season to taste with salt and pepper.

Serve at room temperature. The romesco will keep in the fridge for up to 1 week.

Sambal is a chilli-based sauce popular in many countries across South-East Asia, especially Malaysia, Indonesia and Singapore. It's a fragrant accompaniment to fried fish dishes and dry curries.

Sambal

MAKES ABOUT 500 G (1 LB 2 OZ)

3 bunches coriander (cilantro), roots only, washed well
1 tablespoon shrimp paste
125 g (4½ oz) mild dried chillies
50 g (1¾ oz) onion, roughly chopped
4–5 cm (1½–2 inch) piece of fresh ginger, peeled and roughly chopped
7 garlic cloves, chopped
35 g (1¼ oz) curry leaves
400 ml (14 fl oz) peanut oil
2 tablespoons tamarind paste
1 tablespoon ground turmeric
1 tablespoon sweet paprika
2 tablespoons chopped palm sugar (jaggery)

Place the coriander roots in a blender or food processor. Add the shrimp paste, chillies, onion, ginger, garlic, curry leaves and peanut oil and blend to a paste.

Pour the mixture into a saucepan and cook over medium heat for 20 minutes.

Stir in the remaining ingredients and continue to cook for a further 10 minutes. Remove from the heat and leave to cool.

Store in a sterilised jar in the refrigerator; the sambal will keep for 2–3 weeks.

Sugar syrups will keep in the fridge in a sterilised jar for up to 3 months. The glucose in the second sugar syrup below helps the freezing process and gives sorbets a smooth, rounded consistency.

Sugar syrup (plain)

MAKES 400 ML (14 FL OZ)

250 g (9 oz) caster (superfine) sugar

Put the sugar in a saucepan with 250 ml (9 fl oz/1 cup) water. Place over medium heat and bring to the boil, stirring to dissolve the sugar. Remove from the heat and leave to cool. Store in a clean airtight jar in the fridge.

Sugar syrup for sorbets

MAKES 600 ML (21 FL OZ)

250 g (9 oz) caster (superfine) sugar
125 g (4½ oz) liquid glucose

Put the sugar and glucose in a saucepan with 250 ml (9 fl oz/1 cup) water. Place over medium heat and bring to the boil, stirring to dissolve the sugar. Remove from the heat and leave to cool. Store in a clean airtight jar in the fridge.

The combination of tapioca and rice flour makes this a relatively light batter, perfect for deep-frying oysters and seafood.

Tempura batter

MAKES ABOUT 750 ML (3 CUPS)

150 g (5½ oz) tapioca flour
150 g (5½ oz) rice flour
¼ cup ice cubes
juice of 1 lime
juice of 1 lemon
250 ml (9 fl oz/1 cup) soda water (club soda)

Combine the tapioca flour and rice flour in a bowl. Add the ice cubes, lime juice, lemon juice and soda water, mixing with a fork to form a batter — a few little lumps are fine, as they will crisp up in the deep-fryer.

Make the batter just before you need to use it, or the batter will become flat.

I love making my own relish, and this one is another of my mum's recipes. We used to make big batches of it when tomatoes were cheap. It's so good on steak sandwiches, and nothing like the supermarket variety.

Tomato relish

MAKES ABOUT 1 KG (2 LB 4 OZ)

100 ml (3½ fl oz) extra virgin olive oil
500 g (1 lb 2 oz) brown onions, sliced
1.5 kg (3 lb 5 oz) ripe tomatoes, diced
440 g (15 oz/2 cups) caster (superfine) sugar
2 tablespoons sea salt
3 teaspoons mild curry spice
½ teaspoon chilli powder
1 tablespoon dry mustard powder
500 ml (17 fl oz/2 cups) brown vinegar

Heat the olive oil in a saucepan over medium heat. Add the onion and cook for 7–9 minutes, until softened. Stir in the remaining ingredients and bring to the boil.

Reduce the heat to low and cook, stirring occasionally to stop the mixture sticking to the pan, until the sauce is the consistency of a thick relish. Leave to cool slightly, then pour into warm sterilised jars.

The relish will keep in the fridge for 1 week. Bring to room temperature for serving.

Wasabi paste can be found in Asian grocery stores, or these days even in good supermarkets. This dressing is great with oysters, prawns and sashimi.

Wasabi dressing

MAKES 300 ML (10 FL OZ)

1 tablespoon wasabi paste
2 teaspoons sesame oil
250 ml (9 fl oz/1 cup) olive oil
1 tablespoon soy sauce

Place the wasabi paste in a bowl with 3 tablespoons hot water and whisk until combined.

Gradually add the sesame oil and olive oil, whisking constantly. Add the soy sauce and continue whisking until the mixture has emulsified.

Store in a clean airtight jar in the fridge. The dressing will keep for up to 2 weeks; give it a good shake before using.

Index

Ajvar 143
anchovies, Marinated, on
    sourdough with pico de gallo
    110, **107**
apple
    Apple & ginger purée 129
    Apple jelly 87, **91**
    Apple & walnut bread 32
    Calvados custards with brown
        butter crumble & sauternes 210
asparagus, Soft-boiled eggs
    with truffle salt, sourdough
    soldiers & 36
avocado
    DIY guacamole 71, **68**
    Spicy salmon with curry
        dressing, pear, frozen avocado
        & horseradish 93, **90**

Bacon & egg tacos 21, **19**
Bacon-wrapped scallops with
    green tomato chutney &
    blackened lime 142, **138**
Baked spicy chicken drumettes
    with romesco 170
banana
    Banana parfait with peanut
        brittle & salted caramel
        sauce 214
    Banana salsa 156–7, **158–9**
    Beer-battered bananas
        203, **204–5**
    Caramelised banana 196–7, **198**
    Toasted apple & walnut bread
        with ricotta, smashed banana
        & fresh honeycomb 32
Barbecue sauce 155
batter
    Beer batter 203, **204–5**
    Chickpea batter 88, **90**
    Tempura batter 232
beef
    Beef short ribs with Pedro Ximénez,
        roasted red onion & carrot
        & cumin purée 140–1, **139**
    Grass-fed beef sliders 166

Grilled ox beef tongue with
    ajvar & dill pickle 143
Mini corned beef & crab
    sandwiches 133
Mini hot dogs with kimchi,
    American mustard & chipotle
    mayo 160
Spiced grass-fed beef tartare
    with almonds & sultanas
    136, **139**
Thai beef koftas in lettuce cups
    with coconut sauce 148
Wagyu bresaola bruschetta
    with stracciatella, blood plum
    & fennel cress 149
Beer-battered bananas with
    fresh honeycomb & pandan
    ice cream 203, **204–5**
beetroot
    Beetroot hummus 78
    Beetroot relish 111
    Honey & oregano haloumi with
        fig, golden beets, dandelion &
        walnuts 78
berries
    Roasted nut & quinoa granola
        with coconut, honey &
        berries 35
    Soft Swiss meringue with berries
        & almond anglaise 222–3, **221**
    See also raspberries, strawberries
Blood sausage with pipis, romesco
    & padrón peppers 150
Bounty bars 213
Brandy snap cigars with
    strawberry cream 206, **205**
bread
    Apple & walnut bread 32
    Fried bread 122–3, **124–5**
    Fruit & nut bread 55
    Spinach parathas 49
    Truffled mushroom & pecorino
        flatbreads 44–5, **43**
Brown butter crumble 210
bruschetta, Wagyu bresaola, with
    stracciatella, blood plum &
    fennel cress 149

burgers, Grass-fed beef 166
Buttermilk dressing 178–9

cabbage
    Cabbage kimchi 225
    Cabbage salad 185
    Vietnamese slaw 112
Cabernet sauvignon dressing 226
cakes
    Apple & walnut bread 32
    Pistachio & chocolate cake
        with red wine & coffee-braised
        quince 200–1, **199**
    Calvados custards with brown
        butter crumble & sauternes
        apple 210
capsicum
    Ajvar 143
    Blood sausage with pipis,
        romesco & padrón peppers 150
    Olive & capsicum jam
        186–7, **188–9**
    Red pepper jam 122–3, **124–5**
caramel
    Caramel ice cream 196–7, **198**
    Dulce de leche 218–19, **220**
    Salted caramel sauce 214
carrot
    Carrot & cumin purée 140–1, **139**
    Carrot & daikon salad 182
    Vietnamese slaw 112
cashews, Sugar & spice 59
cauliflower
    Moroccan cauliflower salad
        with saffron yoghurt, pine nuts
        & currants 72
    Piccalilli 108–9, **106**
cavolo nero, Creamed 92, **91**
Celeriac & chorizo frittata with
    jamón & corn salsa 17
cheesecakes, My friend Mario's
    baked maple 208–9
cheese, Fresh, with rosemary 118–19
Chermoula lamb loin with
    pumpkin couscous & harissa
    yoghurt 144

Cherry sorbet 218–19, **220**
chia custards, Chilled, with
chopped fruit, pistachios
& coconut yoghurt 20, **18**
chicken
Baked spicy chicken drumettes
with romesco 170
Chicken garam masala with
raita & tomato & onion salad
174, **177**
Chicken katsu sandwiches with
shaved cabbage salad 185
Crispy salt & pepper popcorn
chicken 81
Rustic chicken pâté with pear
& shallot relish 175, **177**
Spicy soy, ginger & sesame
chicken wings 181
Tandoori-roasted drumsticks
with cucumber, chilli &
coriander salad 180, **176**
chickpeas
Beetroot hummus 78
Chickpea batter 88, **90**
Crispy fried chickpeas 75
Moroccan cauliflower salad
with saffron yoghurt, pine nuts
& currants 72
Salad of roasted pumpkin,
chorizo, chickpeas, quinoa &
blue cheese 66, **69**
Chilled chia custards with
chopped fruit, pistachios
& coconut yoghurt 20, **18**
chilli
Chilli salt 64
Chipotle mayonnaise 226
Nam jim dressing 95
Sambal 231
chocolate
Bounty bars 213
Chocolate sable 218–19, **220**
Chocolate sponge 200–1
Chocolate sweet pastry
196–7, **198**
Gooey chocolate tarts with
caramelised banana &
caramel ice cream 196–7, **198**
Pistachio & chocolate cake
with red wine & coffee-braised
quince 200–1, **199**
Salted chocolate honeycomb 194
Vegan dark chocolate & coconut
tart 202, **204–5**

chorizo
Celeriac & chorizo frittata with
jamón & corn salsa
Chorizo jam 118–19
Grilled chorizo & octopus with
piquillo peppers & apple &
ginger purée 129
Homemade chorizos 152, 152–3
Salad of roasted pumpkin,
chorizo, chickpeas, quinoa &
blue cheese 66, **69**
chutney, Green tomato 229
Cinnamon sugar 26–7
Cocktail sauce 133
coconut
Bounty bars 213
Coconut jackfruit curry
156–7, **158–9**
Coconut panna cotta with
marinated pineapple, pink
peppercorns & fennel 217
Coconut whipped cream 202
Vegan dark chocolate &
coconut tart 202, **204–5**
Confit duck & mustard fruit cigars
with watercress & olive &
coriander salad, Cucumber, chilli
& 180
Corn salsa 17, 30–1, 105
corned beef & crab sandwiches,
Mini 133
couscous, Pumpkin 144
crab
Devilled snow crab on toast 100
Mini corned beef & crab
sandwiches 133
Creamed cavolo nero 92, **91**
Creamed chard 23
Crisp shallots & garlic 227
Crispy bacon & egg tacos with pico
de gallo & kimchi mayo 21, **19**
Crispy fried chickpeas 75
Crispy salt & pepper popcorn
chicken 81
Crisp zucchini flowers with goat's
cheese & salsa verde 70, **69**
croquettes, Salt cod, with piccalilli
108–9, **106**
Crumbed parsnip with remoulade
sauce 67, **68**
crumpets 40, **42**
Macadamia & zucchini fritters
with smoked salmon & corn
salsa 30–1, **18**

Toasted crumpets with salmon
gravlax, feta, cucumber &
horseradish 37
cucumber
Cucumber, chilli & coriander
salad 180
Cucumber pickle 178–9, **176**
Spiced cucumber 103
Curried kale, sweet potato,
caramelised onion & mozzarella
jaffles 29
Curry dressing 227
custard 26–7
Almond anglaise 222–3, **221**
Calvados custards with brown
butter crumble 210
Maldivian baked custard with
persimmon & pomegranate 212

daikon
Carrot & daikon salad 182
Miso daikon 86
Sashimi of kingfish with miso
daikon, apple & coriander 86
Vietnamese slaw 112
dates, in Vegan dark chocolate
& coconut tart 202, **204–5**
Devilled snow crab on toast 100
DIY guacamole 71, **68**
Doughnuts with custard & jam
filling 26–7
duck
Confit duck & mustard fruit
cigars with watercress & olive
& capsicum jam 186–7, **188–9**
Duck prosciutto with sliced
peach, toasted walnuts &
elderflower dressing 173
Salt & sugar-cured duck breast
with sichuan pepper, turnip &
tamarillo glaze 190–1
Dulce de leche 218–19, **220**

eggplant
Ajvar 143
Smoky eggplant 88, **90**
eggs
Celeriac & chorizo frittata with
jamón & corn salsa 17
Crispy bacon & egg tacos
with pico de gallo & kimchi
mayo 21, **19**

Macadamia & zucchini fritters with smoked salmon & corn salsa 30–1, **18**
Quail eggs benedict 13
Shakshuka (eggs baked in tomato sauce) with spinach parathas 24
Smashed spiced pumpkin & ricotta on rye with poached eggs 16, **19**
Soft-boiled eggs with asparagus, truffle salt & sourdough soldiers 36
Elderflower dressing 173
empanadas, Spiced lamb, with tomato chutney & basil mayo 134
English muffins 54
English muffins with swordfish, spiced cucumber & watercress 103
Quail eggs benedict with chilli kale on mini muffins 13

fennel
Fennel & blood orange salad 104, **107**
Kohlrabi & fennel salad 121
feta, Samosas of curried pumpkin & 63
figs, Honey & oregano haloumi with 78
Focaccia three ways 50, **52–3**
Fontina mash 228
Fresh cheese with rosemary 118–19
Fried bread 122–3, **124–5**
frittata, Celeriac & chorizo with jamón & corn salsa 17
fritters
Beer-battered bananas 203, **204–5**
Macadamia & zucchini fritters 30–1, **18**
Salt cod croquettes with piccalilli 108–9, **106**
Whitebait fritters 111
Fruit & nut bread 55
Fruit salad 20, **18**

garfish, Grilled, with kohlrabi & fennel salad 121
garlic
Crisp shallots & garlic 227

Garlic aioli 228
Garlic chilli oil 75
Garlic confit 229
Glazed pork spare ribs 155
goat's cheese
Crisp zucchini flowers with goat's cheese & salsa verde 70, **69**
Focaccia three ways 50, **52–3**
Gooey chocolate tarts with caramelised banana & caramel ice cream 196–7, **198**
Gorgonzola cream 64
Grass-fed beef sliders 166
Green tomato chutney 229
Grilled beef ox tongue with ajvar & dill pickle 143
Grilled chorizo & octopus with piquillo peppers & apple & ginger purée 129
Grilled garfish with kohlrabi & fennel salad 121
Grilled sardines with green tomato chutney & radish salad 126
Guacamole 71, **68**

halmoumi, Honey & oregano, with fig, golden beets, dandelion & walnuts 78
ham
Celeriac & chorizo frittata with jamón & corn salsa 17
Quail eggs benedict 13
Smoked ham, tomato, creamed chard & gruyère toasties 23
hazelnuts
Fruit & nut bread 55
Romesco sauce 231
Herb-crumbed oysters with leek & tartare sauce 96–7
Hollandaise sauce 13
Homemade chorizos 152–3
Homemade merguez sausages 162–3
honey
Honey & oregano haloumi with fig, golden beets, dandelion & walnuts 78
Honey thyme dressing 14
Honey mustard mayo 23
Honeycomb 196–7, **198**
Salted chocolate honeycomb 194

hot dogs, Mini, with kimchi, American mustard & chipotle mayo 160
hummus, Beetroot 78

ice cream
Banana parfait 214
Caramel ice cream 196–7, **198**
Pandan ice cream 203, **204–5**
Peanut butter ice-cream sandwiches 218–19, **220**

jackfruit curry, Coconut 156–7, **158–9**
jaffles, Curried kale, sweet potato, caramelised onion & mozzarella 29
jams
Chorizo jam 118–19
Olive & capsicum jam 186–7, **188–9**
Red pepper jam 122–3, **124–5**
Rhubarb & vanilla jam 26
romesco & chorizo jam 118–19

kale
Chilli kale 13
Curried kale, sweet potato, caramelised onion & mozzarella jaffles 29
Katsu sauce 185
Kimchi 225
Kimchi mayonnaise 21, **19**
kingfish
Kingfish sashimi with nam jim, lime leaf, coconut yoghurt & toasted jasmine rice 95
Sashimi of kingfish with miso daikon, apple & coriander 86
Kohlrabi & fennel salad 121

lamb
Chermoula lamb loin with pumpkin couscous & harissa yoghurt 144
Homemade merguez sausages 162–3
Lamb in puff pastry with mushroom duxelles & dried black olives 147

Lamb neck adobo with coconut jackfruit curry & banana salsa 156–7, **158–9**
Moroccan lamb cutlets with raisin & caper purée, broccolini & hazelnuts 137, **139**
Spiced lamb empanadas with tomato chutney & basil mayo 134
Lavender cream 207
leek & tartare sauce, Herb-crumbed oysters with 96–7
lobster & Vietnamese slaw, Milk buns with 112

Macadamia & zucchini fritters with smoked salmon & corn salsa 30–1, **18**
Maldivian baked custard with persimmon & pomegranate 212
maple cheesecakes, My friend Mario's baked 208–9
Marinated anchovies on sourdough with pico de gallo 110, **107**
Marinated pineapple 217
meatballs, Sumac-spiced pork & veal, with fontina mash 165
meringue, Soft Swiss, with berries & almond anglaise 222–3
Milk buns with lobster & Vietnamese slaw 112
Mini corned beef & crab sandwiches 133
Mini hot dogs with kimchi, American mustard & chipotle mayo 160
Mini pistachio crème brûlée tarts 207, **204**
Miso mayo 230
Moroccan cauliflower salad with saffron yoghurt, pine nuts & currants 72
Moroccan lamb cutlets with raisin & caper purée, broccolini & hazelnuts 137, **139**
muesli, toasted 35
muffins, English 54
English muffins with swordfish, spiced cucumber & watercress 103
Quail eggs benedict with chilli kale on mini muffins 13

mushrooms
Lamb in puff pastry with mushroom duxelles & dried black olives 147
Mushroom duxelles 44–5, 147
Truffled mushroom & pecorino flatbreads 44–5, **43**
mussel po boys, Tempura 122–3, **124–5**
My friend Mario's baked maple cheesecakes 208–9

Nam jim dressing 95
Natural oysters with apple jelly, pernod tapioca, salmon caviar & chives 87, **91**
nuts
Fruit & nut bread 55
Toasted granola 35
See also specific nuts

octopus with piquillo peppers & apple & ginger purée, Grilled chorizo & 129
Olive & capsicum jam 186–7, **188–9**
onion
Onion confit 230
Pancetta & onion tarts 14
Potato, caramelised onion, fig, gorgonzola & grilled radicchio pizzas 46–7, **43**
Roasted red onion 140–1, **139**
Tomato & onion salad 174, **176**
ox tongue with ajvar & dill pickle, Grilled 143
oysters
Cabbage kimchi 225
Herb-crumbed oysters with leek & tartare sauce 96–7
Natural oysters with apple jelly, pernod tapioca, salmon caviar & chives 87, **91**
Oysters in chickpea batter with smoky eggplant & tzatziki 88, **90**
Tempura oysters with wakame salad, nori & wasabi 84

pancetta
Bacon-wrapped scallops with green tomato chutney & blackened lime 142, **138**

Pancetta & onion tarts 14
panna cotta, Coconut, with marinated pineapple, pink peppercorns & fennel 217
parathas, Spinach 49
parfait, Peanut butter 218–19, **220**
parmesan cheese
Focaccia three ways 50, **52–3**
Truffle oil, parmesan & chive popcorn 60
parsnip, Crumbed 67, **68**
pastries
Duck & mustard fruit cigars 186–7, **188–9**
Gooey chocolate tarts 196–7
Lamb in puff pastry with mushroom duxelles & dried black olives 147
Pancetta & onion tarts 14
Spiced lamb empanadas 134
pastry
Chocolate sable 218–19, **220**
Chocolate sweet pastry 196–7, **198**
Patatas bravas with spicy sauce & garlic aioli 77
peach, Duck prosciutto with toasted walnuts, elderflower dressing & 173
peanuts
Peanut brittle 214
Peanut butter ice-cream sandwiches 218–19, **220**
Pear & shallot relish 175, **177**
persimmon & pomegranate, Maldivian baked custard with 212
Piccalilli 108–9, **106**
pickles
Cucumber pickle 178–9, **176**
Piccalilli 108–9, **106**
Pico de gallo 21, 110, **19**, **107**
pineapple
Marinated pineapple 217
Pineapple salsa 116
pipis, romesco & padrón peppers, Blood sausage with 150
pistachios
Mini pistachio crème brûlée tarts 207, **204**
Pistachio & chocolate cake with red wine & coffee-braised quince 200–1, **199**
Pistachio mousse 200–1
Toasted granola 35

pizza
    Focaccia three ways 50, **52–3**
    Potato, caramelised onion, fig,
      gorgonzola & grilled radicchio
      pizzas 46–7, **43**
pomegranate, Maldivian baked
    custard with persimmon & 212
popcorn
    Spicy popcorn 76
    Truffle oil, parmesan & chive
      popcorn 60
popovers, Rosemary, with
    seaweed butter 41, **42**
pork
    Glazed pork spare ribs 155
    Homemade chorizos 152
    Sumac-spiced pork & veal
      meatballs with fontina mash 165
potatoes
    Fontina mash 228
    Patatas bravas with spicy sauce
      & garlic aioli 77
    Potato, caramelised onion, fig,
      gorgonzola & grilled radicchio
      pizzas 46–7, **43**
    Salt cod croquettes with
      piccalilli 108–9, **106**
prawns
    Prawn toasts with smoked corn
      salsa & chipotle 105, **106**
    Split prawns with a garlic, dashi,
      chilli & lime butter 115
    Tempura prawn tortillas with
      pineapple salsa & chipotle
      mayo 116
prosciutto, Duck, with sliced
    peach, toasted walnuts &
    elderflower dressing 173
pumpkin
    Pumpkin couscous 144
    Salad of roasted pumpkin,
      chorizo, chickpeas, quinoa &
      blue cheese 66, **69**
    Samosas of curried pumpkin &
      feta 63
    Smashed spiced pumpkin 16, **19**

quail
    Southern-style quail with
      buttermilk dressing &
      cucumber pickle 178–9, **176**
    Tempura quail with carrot &
      daikon salad & wasabi 182

Quail eggs benedict with chilli
    kale on mini muffins 13
quince, Red wine & coffee-braised
    200–1, **199**
quinoa
    Roasted nut & quinoa granola
      with coconut, honey & berries 35
    Salad of roasted pumpkin,
      chorizo, chickpeas, quinoa &
      blue cheese 66, **69**

Radish salad 126
raisins
    Fruit & nut bread 55
    Raisin & caper purée 137, **139**
raspberries
    My friend Mario's baked maple
      cheesecakes 208–9
    Raspberries coulis 222–3, **221**
    Soft Swiss meringue with berries
      & almond anglaise 222–3, **221**
Raw tuna pizzettas with cavolo
    nero, yellow tomatoes,
    jalapeño & wasabi 92, **91**
Red pepper jam 122–3, **124–5**
Red wine & coffee-braised quince
    200–1, **199**
relishes
    Beetroot relish 111
    Pear & shallot relish 175, **177**
    Tomato relish 233
Rhubarb & vanilla jam 26–7
ricotta cheese
    Smashed spiced pumpkin &
      ricotta on rye with poached
      eggs 16, **19**
    Toasted apple & walnut bread
      with ricotta, smashed banana
      & fresh honeycomb 32
Roasted nut & quinoa granola with
    coconut, honey & berries 35
Romesco sauce 231
Rosemary popovers with seaweed
    butter 41, **42**
Rustic chicken pâté with pear &
    shallot relish 175, **177**

salads
    Cabbage salad 185
    Carrot & daikon salad 182
    Cucumber, chilli & coriander
      salad 180

Fennel & blood orange salad
    104, **107**
Kohlrabi & fennel salad 121
Moroccan cauliflower salad
    with saffron yoghurt, pine nuts
    & currants 72
Radish salad 126
Salad of roasted pumpkin,
    chorizo, chickpeas, quinoa &
    blue cheese 66, **69**
Tomato & onion salad 174, **176**
Vietnamese slaw 112
salmon
    Salmon gravlax 37
    smoked salmon, Macadamia &
      zucchini fritters with corn salsa
      & 30–1, **18**
    Spicy salmon with curry
      dressing, pear, frozen avocado
      & horseradish 93, **90**
Salsa verde 70, **69**
Salt cod croquettes with piccalilli
    108–9, **106**
Salted chocolate honeycomb 194
Salt & sugar-cured duck breast
    with sichuan pepper, turnip &
    tamarillo glaze 190–1
Sambal 231
Samosas of curried pumpkin &
    feta with mint & lime yoghurt 63
sandwiches
    Chicken katsu sandwiches with
      shaved cabbage salad 185
    Mini corned beef & crab
      sandwiches 133
sardines, Grilled, with green tomato
    chutney & radish salad 126
Sashimi of kingfish with miso
    daikon, apple & coriander 86
sausages
    Blood sausage with pipis,
      romesco & padrón peppers 150
    Homemade merguez sausages
      162–3
    Mini hot dogs with kimchi,
      American mustard & chipotle
      mayo 160
scallops
    Bacon-wrapped scallops with
      green tomato chutney &
      blackened lime 142, **138**
    Seared scallops with padrón
      peppers, fresh cheese,
      romesco & chorizo jam 118–19

Seaweed butter 41

Shakshuka (eggs baked in tomato sauce) with spinach parathas 24

shallot
Crisp shallots & garlic 227
Pear & shallot relish 175, **177**

silverbeet (chard), Creamed 23

sliders, Grass-fed beef 166

Smashed spiced pumpkin & ricotta on rye with poached eggs 16, **19**

Smoked ham, tomato, creamed chard & gruyère toasties 23

Smoky eggplant 88, **90**

Soft-boiled eggs with asparagus, truffle salt & sourdough soldiers 36

Soft Swiss meringue with berries & almond anglaise 222–3

Southern-style quail with buttermilk dressing & cucumber pickle 178–9, **176**

Spiced cucumber 103

Spiced grass-fed beef tartare with almonds & sultanas 136, **139**

Spiced lamb empanadas with tomato chutney & basil mayo 134

Spicy popcorn 76

Spicy salmon with curry dressing, pear, frozen avocado & horseradish 93, **90**

Spicy soy, ginger & sesame chicken wings 181

Spicy tomato sauce 77

Spinach parathas 49

Split prawns with a garlic, dashi, chilli & lime butter 115

stilton, Salad of roasted pumpkin, chorizo, chickpeas, quinoa & 66, **69**

stracciatella, Wagyu bresaola bruschetta with 149

strawberries
Brandy snap cigars with strawberry cream 206, **205**
Soft Swiss meringue with berries & almond anglaise 222–3, **221**
Strawberry jus 218–19, **220**

Sugar & spice cashews 59

Sugar syrup for sorbets 232

Sugar syrup (plain) 232

Sumac-spiced pork & veal meatballs with fontina mash 165

sweet potatoes
Curried kale, sweet potato, caramelised onion & mozzarella jaffles 29
Sweet potato & chilli salt fries with gorgonzola cream 64

swordfish, spiced cucumber & watercress, English muffins with 103

tacos, Crispy bacon & egg, with pico de gallo & kimchi mayo 21, **19**

Tamarillo glaze 190–1

Tandoori-roasted drumsticks with cucumber, chilli & coriander salad 180, **176**

tapioca, Pernod 87, **91**

Tartare sauce 96–7

tarts
Mini pistachio crème brûlée tarts 207, **204**
Pancetta & onion tarts 14
Vegan dark chocolate & coconut tart 202, **204–5**

Tempura batter 232

Tempura mussel po boys 122–3, **124–5**

Tempura oysters with wakame salad, nori & wasabi 84

Tempura prawn tortillas with pineapple salsa & chipotle mayo 116

Tempura quail with carrot & daikon salad & wasabi 182

Thai beef koftas in lettuce cups with coconut sauce 148

Toasted apple & walnut bread with ricotta, smashed banana & fresh honeycomb 32

Toasted crumpets with salmon gravlax, feta, cucumber & horseradish 37

tomato
Green tomato chutney 229
Piccalilli 108–9, **106**
Pico de gallo 21, 110, **19, 107**
Romesco sauce 231
Shakshuka (eggs baked in tomato sauce) 24
Smoked ham, tomato, creamed chard & gruyère toasties 23
Spicy tomato sauce 77

Tomato & onion salad 174, **176**

Tomato relish 233

Tomato sauce 165

tongue, Grilled ox, with ajvar & dill pickle 143

tortillas, Tempura prawn, with pineapple salsa & chipotle mayo 116

Truffled mushroom & pecorino flatbreads 44–5, **43**

Truffle oil, parmesan & chive popcorn 60

tuna, Raw, pizzettas with cavolo nero, yellow tomatoes, jalapeño & wasabi 92, **91**

Turmeric & semolina-crusted whiting with fennel & blood orange salad 104, **107**

Tzatziki 88, **90**

veal meatballs, Sumac-spiced pork & 165

Vegan dark chocolate & coconut tart 202, **204–5**

Vietnamese slaw 112

Wagyu bresaola bruschetta with stracciatella, blood plum & fennel cress 149

walnuts
Apple & walnut bread 32
Duck prosciutto with sliced peach, toasted walnuts & elderflower dressing 173
Fruit & nut bread 55
Honey & oregano haloumi with fig, golden beets, dandelion & walnuts 78
Toasted granola 35

Wasabi dressing 233

Whitebait fritters with beetroot relish & dill crème fraîche 111

whiting, Turmeric & semolina-crusted, with fennel & blood orange salad 104, **107**

zucchini fritters, Macadamia &, with smoked salmon & corn salsa 30–1, **18**

zucchini flowers, Crisp, with goat's cheese & salsa verde 70, **69**

Published in 2017 by Murdoch Books, an imprint of Allen & Unwin

Murdoch Books Australia
83 Alexander Street, Crows Nest NSW 2065
Phone: +61 (0)2 8425 0100
murdochbooks.com.au
info@murdochbooks.com.au

Murdoch Books UK
Ormond House, 26–27 Boswell Street,
London WC1N 3JZ
Phone: +44 (0) 20 8785 5995
murdochbooks.co.uk
info@murdochbooks.co.uk

For corporate orders and custom publishing contact our business development team at
salesenquiries@murdochbooks.com.au

Publisher: Corinne Roberts
Designer: Hugh Ford
Editorial Manager: Jane Price
Editor: Katri Hilden
Photographer: Nikki To
Stylist: Lynsey Fyers
Production Manager: Rachel Walsh

ISBN 978 1 74336 922 7 Australia
ISBN 978 1 74336 925 8 UK

A cataloguing-in-publication entry is available from the catalogue
of the National Library of Australia at nla.gov.au
A catalogue record for this book is available from the British Library

Colour reproduction by Splitting Image Colour Studio Pty Ltd, Clayton, Victoria
Printed by Hang Tai Printing Company, China

MEASURES GUIDE: We have used 20 ml (4 teaspoon) tablespoon measures. If you are using a 15 ml
(3 teaspoon) tablespoon add an extra teaspoon of the ingredient for each tablespoon specified.

IMPORTANT: Those who might be at risk from the effects of salmonella poisoning (the elderly, pregnant
women, young children and those suffering from immune deficiency diseases) should consult their
doctor with any concerns about eating raw or lightly cooked eggs.